# Soccer Systems & Strategies

## Jens Bangsbo

## Birger Peitersen

**Human Kinetics**

**Library of Congress Cataloging-in-Publication Data**

Bangsbo, J. (Jens)
   Soccer systems and strategies / Jens Bangsbo, Birger Peitersen.
     p.   cm.
   ISBN 0-7360-0300-2
     1. Soccer.   2. Soccer--Coaching.   I. Peitersen, Birger.   II. Title.
   GV943.B39   2000
   796.334'2--dc21                                 00-020657

ISBN: 0-7360-0300-2

This book is a revised edition of *Det Gode Hold,* published in 1997 by Danmarks Højskole for Legemsøvelser and Forlaget Hovedland.

**Acquisitions Editor**: Jeff Riley; **Managing Editor**: Leigh LaHood; **Assistant Editor**: Kim Thoren; **Copyeditor**: Marc Jennings; **Proofreader**: Laura Ward Majersky; **Graphic Designer**: Nancy Rasmus; **Graphic Artist**: Sandra Meier; **Cover Designer**: Jack W. Davis; **Photographer (cover)**: Photo Run/ Victah Sailer © 1997; **Photographers (interior)**: Photos on pages x and 48 © Frank DiBrango, photo on page 56 © John Todd/SportsChrome USA, photo on page 86 © Bongarts/SportsChrome USA, all other photos © Per Kjaerbye Pressefotograf; **Illustrator**: Kristin King; **Printer**: United Graphics

On the cover, American midfielder Jeff Agoos (left) battles a Mexican defender for possession in a 1997 World Cup qualifier match. The Americans tied Mexico, 0-0, in front of 114,600 fans—marking the first time in the 63-year history of the USA–Mexico series that the Americans earned, at most, a tie in Mexico City.

Human Kinetics books are available at special discounts for bulk purchase. Special editions or book excerpts can also be created to specification. For details, contact the Special Sales Manager at Human Kinetics.

Printed in the United States of America

10  9  8  7  6  5  4  3  2  1

**Human Kinetics**
Web site: http://www.humankinetics.com/

*United States:* Human Kinetics
P.O. Box 5076, Champaign, IL 61825-5076
1-800-747-4457
e-mail: humank@hkusa.com

*Canada:* Human Kinetics
475 Devonshire Road Unit 100, Windsor, ON N8Y 2L5
1-800-465-7301 (in Canada only)
e-mail: humank@hkcanada.com

*Europe:* Human Kinetics
P.O. Box IW14, Leeds LS16 6TR, United Kingdom
+44 (0)113-278 1708
e-mail: humank@hkeurope.com

*Australia:* Human Kinetics
57A Price Avenue, Lower Mitcham, South Australia 5062
(08) 82771555
e-mail: liahka@senet.com.au

*New Zealand:* Human Kinetics
P.O. Box 105-231, Auckland Central
09-523-3462
e-mail: humank@hknewz.com

# Soccer Systems & Strategies

# CONTENTS

# INTRODUCTION

Every soccer team develops its own methods of attacking and defending. This book describes the process and training that lead to the creation of "the tactically good team."

*Tactics* means action in specific situations, both for the players and for the coach. The players try to play according to the tactical guidelines practiced or decided upon before the match. Central to the coach's role are the abilities both to formulate the team's tactical approach and, according to how the match develops, to make tactical changes.

Denmark's final, decisive World Cup qualifier against Spain in November 1993 is a good example of the demanding yet fascinating challenge of tactics. Denmark needed at least a draw in order to be certain of qualifying for the 1994 World Cup in the United States, while Spain, the home team, needed a win to ensure its participation at the finals. How should the Danish team approach the game tactically? Should Denmark start off with a deep defensive position, the emphasis on utilization of counterplay, or should the team commence play with a forward-looking defense, pressuring into the opposition's half of the pitch? Should the team play with one or two strikers? Should Denmark play with three, four, or five at the back?

After barely 10 minutes of play, Zubizaretta, the Spanish goalkeeper, is sent off. Should this be cause for possible adjustments to the plan? No changes are immediately noticeable, and the Danes seem to gain no advantage through their superiority of numbers. The score at halftime is 0-0. After 18 minutes of play in the second half, the midfield player Hierro scores after a corner kick. If the situation remains as it is, Denmark will not qualify for the World Cup. How can the team turn the game around? What tactical adjustments should the Danes make?

This is a genuine example of some of the tactical challenges a coach should be prepared to tackle before and during a match. The coach evaluates and selects the tactical elements the team should focus on. With the uncertainty of the game and its inherent challenges, there are a number of options to consider when settling on the ideal style of play. The coach makes an evaluation in the light of subjective ideals in the game. One such ideal has been described by Jean-Paul Sartre, the French philosopher.

The key is for the coach to make action-related changes during the match.

He suggests that the course of a soccer match is an exciting event, within whose realms a constant alternation takes place between

- freedom and restriction,
- spontaneity and planning,
- individuality and group dynamics, and
- options and power.

The individual players' options in unpredictable soccer situations veer, therefore, between these pairs of ideas, and a player's actions acquire meaning only when taken as a whole in the context of the actions of the team. The player's reaction has meaning for, and leads to action by, another team member. This develops a strong experience of connection and belonging, which creates a nice, sociable team feeling. The player feels part of a team. "The good team" is one with the ability to find a balance, on both an individual and a team basis, between a predetermined plan and spontaneous action; between the individual player's utilization of personal qualities and group tactics; and an alternation between freedom and restriction according to the team's existing resources.

Not surprisingly, you can identify almost complete harmonic fulfillment of Sartre's analysis when you look back on championship teams. The Danish European Champions of 1992 and the French World Champions of 1998 appeared extremely well balanced and organized at the time.

It is thus of great importance, both on and off the training arena, to work with tactical aspects of the game of soccer. This book provides ideas and inspiration toward that end.

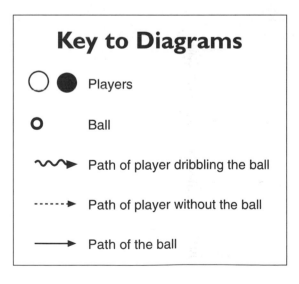

# CHAPTER I

# Systems of Play

Soccer hinges on tactical opportunities and limitations in modes of attacking and defending. Offensive and defensive play consist of different phases depending on where the ball is on the pitch, as illustrated in figure 1.1.

The player's train of thought alternates between offense—"How can I help to keep the ball within the team and bring it forward?"—and defense—"What should I do to help my team regain the ball and to prevent the opposition from scoring?"

## Fundamentals of Systems of Play

A plan called a system of play governs the way players act individually and together with others on the pitch. Such a system consists of a starting formation and guidelines for carrying out the primary functions in attacking and defensive play.

In modern soccer, number combinations identify the systems, showing how many players in the team's opening formation occupy each of the three zones: defense, midfield, and attack. When we talk, say, about the 4-4-2 system, we mean that in the basic formation there are four players in the defensive zone, four players in the midfield area, and two players in the attacking zone. We speak of the back row or defensive unit, the midfield unit, and the attacking unit.

The systems' numeric combinations are relatively uninteresting: it is players who win matches, not systems. Still, the choice of a system of play is tactically important. It is vital to decide upon a combination of figures according to the skills of the players on the roster. The coach should designate players' positions and roles with the idea of giving individual players and the team the best options for maneuvering on both offense and defense.

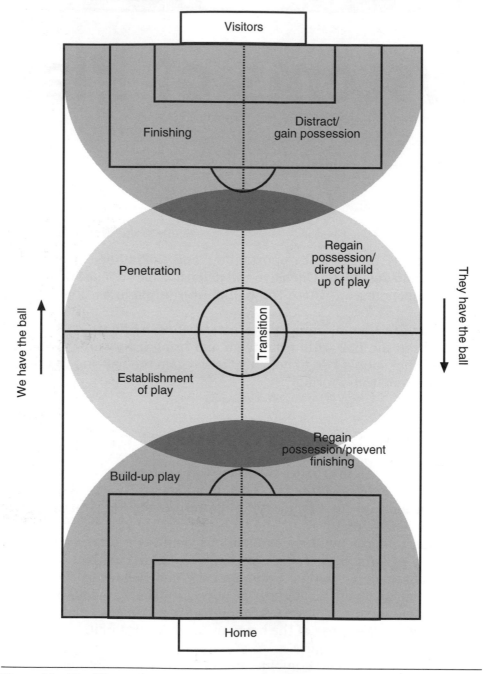

**Figure 1.1**   The different phases of offensive and defensive play.

Changes in styles of play are particularly visible during the World Cup and European Championships.

# Development of Systems of Play

Modern soccer, association soccer, dates back to 1863, when the first national association, the English Football Association, was formed. The association gradually decided upon a set of rules that won common support.

From the mid-1860s up to the present day, a clear thread runs through the organization of the game. In the first international match, between

England and Scotland in 1872, the teams appeared with one goalkeeper, one fullback, one central defender and eight attackers (a 1-1-8 system); many of today's teams appear in a 4-5-1 formation (see figure 1.2). This means that during the 125 or so years since, there has been a marked shift in numbers of players from attack to defense. In the beginning, soccer was a game of dribbling because of the offside rule then, which stated that a player was offside if he was in front of the ball when it was passed. It was not long before this was replaced: a player was offside only on the opposition's half of the pitch and if fewer than three opponents were closer to their own goal line at the moment when the ball was played. In 1925 the offside rule was changed to the present basic rule, that there should be at least two opponents closer to their own goal line at the moment when the ball is played, and from this the game acquired the tactical and technical character we know today.

Systems of play succeeded one another and, slowly, several players were pushed back into the defensive area. From around 1925 to about 1945, Arsenal's system of play set the fashion. It was called the Three-Back system, or the WM system. When the formation was seen from above, the

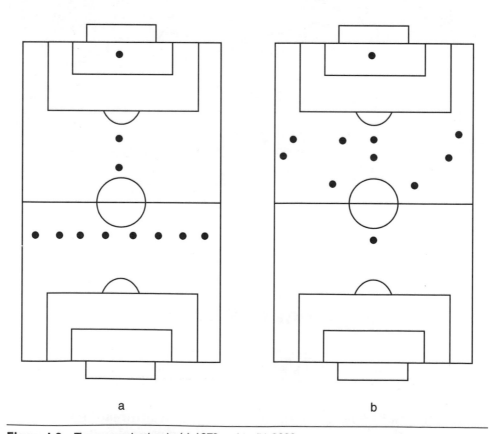

a           b

**Figure 1.2** Team organization in (a) 1872 and in (b) 2000.

attackers formed the letter *W*, while the defenders' lineup displayed the letter *M* (see figure 1.3). Its innovation was that the center half was pushed even further back, in line with the two fullbacks. When the hitherto undefeated English national team was beaten 6-3 by Hungary at Wembley Stadium in 1956, a new system began to make its presence felt. The Hungarians moved the foremost central attacker back down the pitch and utilized the area behind the opposition's markers with quick passes. The system was a 3-3-4 arrangement. That was succeeded by the evolving Brazilian model 4-2-4, which contributed to Brazil's World Cup victory of 1958 (see figure 1.4).

In contrast to the WM system, the Brazilian system created numerical superiority both on the attack and on defense. On the other hand, the system was completely reliant on the two midfielders' physical and tactical abilities. The Brazilian formation ushered in the new age of

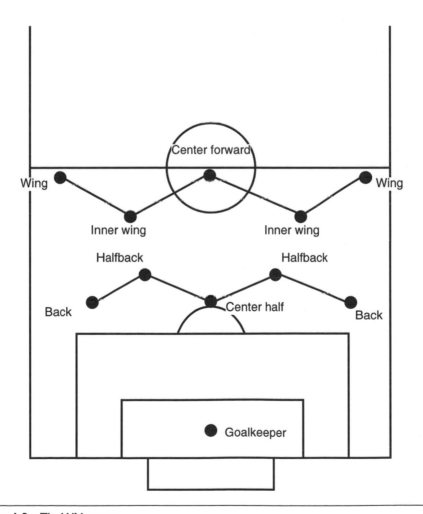

**Figure 1.3**   The WM system.

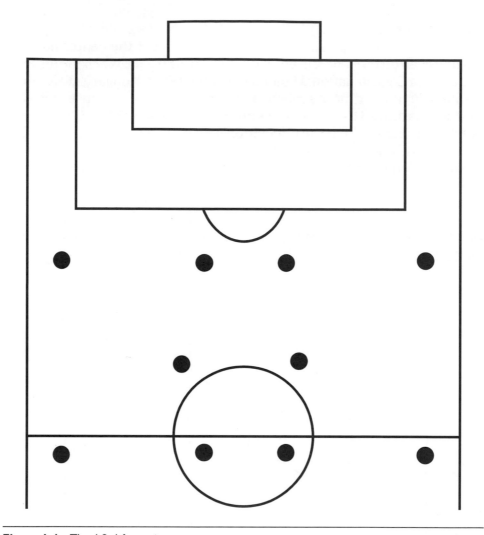

**Figure 1.4** The 4-2-4 formation.

modern systems of play. The earlier positional notations were replaced with new names and the players were positioned in units (defense, midfield, and attack). At the same time, the roles of the players became more flexible.

Both before and after the 1958 World Cup, many Italian teams adhered to an ultradefensive formation called Catenaccio. This defensive tactic evolved as a direct result of the great clubs engaging the best soccer players of the time, such as John Hansen of Denmark. The other teams concentrated on limiting their defeats. They double-marked the star players and placed an extra defender (sweeper) behind the defense, so that the formation became 5-3-2. Other great soccer-playing nations

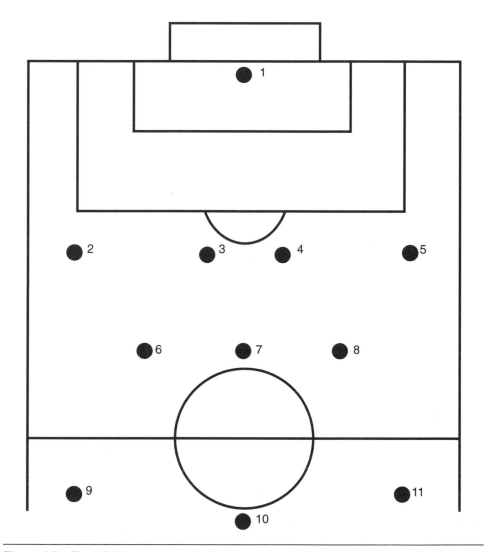

**Figure 1.5**   The 4-3-3 formation.

adjusted the Brazilian arrangement, and England won the 1966 World Cup in the gradually prevailing 4-3-3 formation (see figure 1.5).

Since the mid-1970s, the most common system has been the 4-4-2 formation (see figure 1.6) and, in conjunction with this, new positions have been named. They differ from those of the 1950s and reflect new roles and opportunities. A classic 4-4-2 formation consists of four on defense (two central defenders or one central defender and a libero, plus one left back and one right back), four in the midfield (usually arranged in a diamond shape, with a defensive midfield player, one right and one left midfielder, and one offensive midfield player; see page 18), and two attackers who are forwards. In line with the reduction in number of attackers, some teams

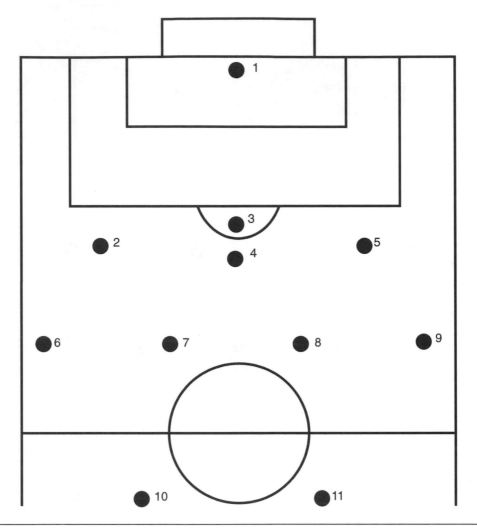

**Figure 1.6** The 4-4-2 formation.

reduced the number of defenders at the back accordingly. Sepp Piontek's successful Danish national team adapted to playing 3-5-2 during the 1980s (see figure 1.7).

The most common systems currently in use are covered in more detail in the following pages. We first describe each system in the abstract, then we refer to a specific team that has used the system successfully. We have

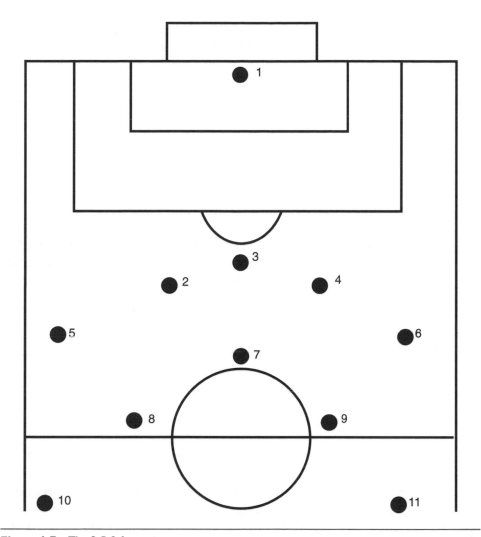

**Figure 1.7**  The 3-5-2 formation.

used internationally famous teams as examples, since the majority of soccer enthusiasts will probably be able to recall the way these clubs played. To conclude the examination and description of the various systems, we have provided a sample training session in one of the main characteristics of each system.

# The 4-3-3 System

**Starting Formation**

Four players in defense, three midfielders, and three attackers (see figure 1.5, p 7).

**Organization**

The defense starts off with either four players in a line or with one player (a sweeper or libero) positioned behind the other three. The midfield can be arranged in two different variations—a linear or a triangular arrangement, offensive or defensive in character (see figure 1.8). The attackers would normally arrange themselves so that the opposition's defense is spread as widely as possible. If the center forward is strong in the air, another of the strikers can also move into the central area during the buildup to exploit the second ball.

**Attacking**

The system, with its three attackers, is offensive in character. The ball should ideally be played quickly up to the strikers so that the game is taken into the opposition's defensive zone. At the same time, support should come quickly from the center of the pitch so that the two sets of players are working together. Passes to the strikers often come from defense. A defender who has been able to create space and time with the ball can try to put a long pass out to the attackers. Depending on the receiving player's position and technical ability, the pass can arrive right at the feet of the player or in a free area behind the opposition's defense. The three attackers should vary their options of receiving the ball among each other so that the opposition is constantly in doubt as to their next movements. If the center forward moves back down the pitch for a pass, the area behind the forward (i.e., further up the pitch) may be used by other midfielders, who are running up from behind. For example, in the 1994 World Championships, Roberto Baggio played as center forward, but he frequently moved back down the pitch, a move his team tactically exploited.

The Dutch national team also made use of this idea in Euro 96. When Kluivert moved back, Bergkamp utilized the free space. A team with a fast winger should also use the free space behind the fullback for an attempt to penetrate the defense and take the opposition by surprise.

The midfield's offensive options depend on the formation. With two advanced midfielders, the scene is set for combination play between the midfield and the attackers. If there is only one offensive

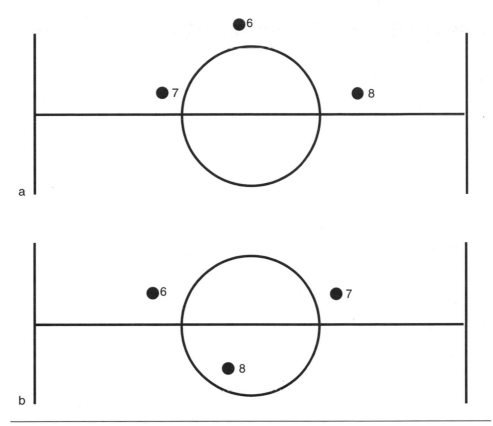

**Figure 1.8**   The midfield can be arranged as either (a) offensive or (b) defensive.

midfielder, that player's most important role is to play the attackers in free spaces for them to finish.

## Defending

The back row is normally organized using zonal marking and with close teamwork between the two central defenders, one of whom is preferably a sweeper. The midfield is the vulnerable area in a team's defensive half, requiring careful organization of the responsibilities of the three players. Most coaches favor a centrally placed midfielder who is strong in close combat and usually stays behind the other two players. Midfield players are often characterized by their well-developed ability to create good consolidation play, where one of them is the designated playmaker.

To assist the midfield, in specific situations a fullback can move forward and out toward the wing in order to seek out an opponent. The attackers have important defensive roles, partly in closing off the wings for the opposition's fullbacks and partly in working as a team to pressure the ball when the opposition controls it in its own defensive zone.

## How Juventus Played 4-3-3 in 1996

### Starting Formation

The Champion's League winners of 1996, Juventus played 4-3-3 in the final against Ajax (see figure 1.9).

### Attacking

In Italy, all talk was of the Juventus trio: Vialli, Del Piero, and Ravanelli. The three possessed offensive qualities that the team exploited by placing them in the front row. There was great reciprocal understanding between their runs and, since all three were strong finishers, they lured defenders with them whenever they moved. A characteristic of the attacking play was the long, high balls forward toward free areas behind the opposition's defense, into which either Ravanelli or Vialli

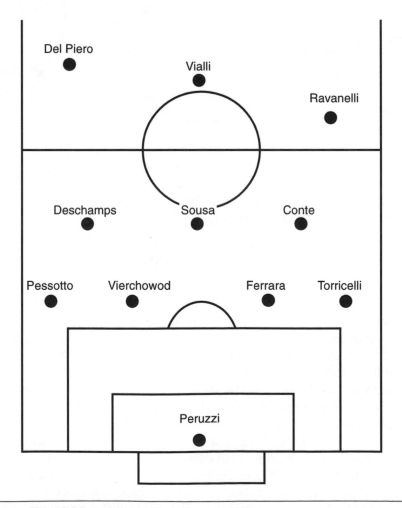

**Figure 1.9**  The 4-3-3 formation used by Juventus in 1996.

would move. Passes were also directed toward Ravanelli's head or chest, while Del Piero and Vialli made breaks, anticipating a pass. Ravanelli and Vialli were physically strong in one-on-one situations and were adept at keeping hold of the ball when outnumbered. This meant that the midfield had the time and the opportunity to get up in attack when the long passes were played from the defense. Conte and Deschamps, among others, used the threat of a long ball when the midfield had pushed up the field.

Apart from the long ball from defense, the two fullbacks were used as buildup players; this was generally in order to create width in

Ravanelli has moved into an open space and has the skills to maintain possession of the ball.

the buildup, but they were also used as players who penetrated the defense. Along the right wing, Torricelli, in particular, made a few breaks where he exploited the fact that the defenders were watching the trio of attackers. He took the opportunity to come forward and finish himself.

### Defending

The back four were organized with two central defenders, who supported each other. The two fullbacks were extremely aggressive in their defensive play, meeting every opponent early; part of the reason for this was to relieve the pressure on the midfield.

The midfield was organized in a line, with balance that was fluid and dynamic. The other two units excellently supported the midfield's work. The strikers shared the depth on the pitch, and the fullbacks quickly harried their opponents. This usually meant that the three midfield players could concentrate on taking charge in the center of midfield. The team was, as a rule, physically strong, and the players understood how to use these physical resources to create close coherence between the units in a 4-3-3 system.

## Sample Training Session Using 4-3-3

Following is an example of how a coach can train a team playing 4-3-3 in one of the system's main characteristics—utilization of the two wingers. See figure 1.10.

### Pitch

One-half pitch with three zones (one to three) and a full-size goal.

### Players

Thirteen—seven white and five black players, and a goalkeeper.

### Description

One of white's midfielders plays the ball into the penalty area, where the goalkeeper takes it and starts a buildup via one of the two fullbacks (number 2 or number 5), who is consciously made available by the white team. Numbers 9, 10, and 11 adapt their relative positions according to the side of the pitch on which the buildup takes place. When the ball is played out, 5 is pursued by 9, the aim being to lure the fullback as far up the pitch as possible. When 5 reaches zone two, 9 may no longer follow him, and two white midfielders attempt to win the ball. If the ball goes to the opposite side, this is designated zone three. In this zone, two white players can take part in winning the ball. As soon as this has been accomplished, the ball is played to the supporting player behind, who, with one touch, plays out to the

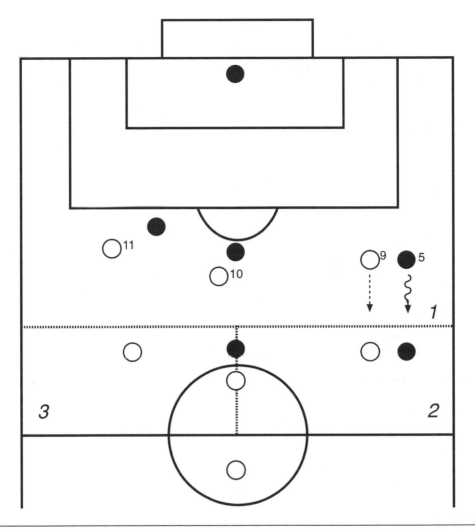

**Figure 1.10**  4-3-3 training session.

free space behind the fullback. At the instant the ball is won, 10 breaks into the free space that has been created and receives a pass. At the same moment, 11 also breaks diagonally, to receive a cross from 10 close to the penalty spot. It is important that the midfielder farthest away break directly forward and move toward the penalty area to receive a cross well inside the box.

### Scoring

Score as normal for the white team; the black team scores by playing the ball over the halfway line in zones two or three. This is accomplished either by dribbling the ball over or by passing it to another member of the team, who receives it on the other side of the halfway line.

## Variations

1. When the ball is passed into the penalty area, the white team may score, while the black team may pass and lay the ball off to the goalkeeper (according to the old rules).
2. Numbers 10 or 11 may be passed to at will.
3. Several players can be added to the game, and the whole of the halfway line becomes the scoring line for the black team.

## Coaching Points

The practice trains players for preparation and utilization of counter-attacks by consciously directing the opposition's buildup. Number 9 should hold back slightly by the side of number 5, so that 5 does not have the opportunity to stop and change the direction of play. Numbers 10 and 11 should expect to utilize the free space created behind 5. Only a short time should elapse between the ball being won and the long pass to 10, and it is therefore important for the supporting players to keep moving, ready for a possible change of possession. They should also ensure that they themselves create a good passing angle both for the player (10), and a good position for the forward passes.

## Keywords

Allow the player to move forward • Quick delivery • Utilize the free space

# The 4-4-2 System

## Starting Formation

Four players in defense, four midfield players, and two attackers (see figure 1.11).

## Organization

Arrange the defensive unit either with four players in a line or with one player (a sweeper) behind the other three. Position the midfield unit in any of several variations: diamond, line, bowl, two-two, and three-one arrangement (see figure 1.12). The two attackers either start off as a pair (i.e., working closely together in the central area) or position themselves on the wings.

### Attacking

The three units' roles in terms of moving should be integrated and complement each other, to utilize width and depth in the game.

In the attacking structure, the two fullbacks should ensure that there is width in the buildup. Space should simultaneously be created for offensive moves up the pitch. This is facilitated if the offensive midfielder moves away from the wing. By doing this, the midfielder creates space for offensive support for the fullbacks and becomes available for the option of a combination. Using this system demands that the fullbacks come forward down the wings in the opposition's defensive zone and, in particular, deliver crosses to the central players. The two fullbacks should be skilled at accessing all situations.

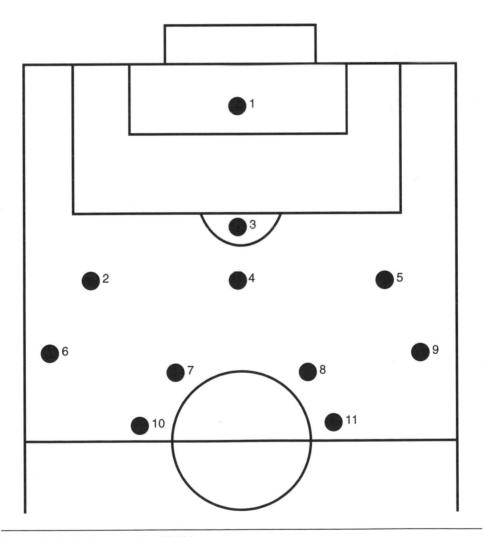

**Figure 1.11**    Defensive and midfield formation.

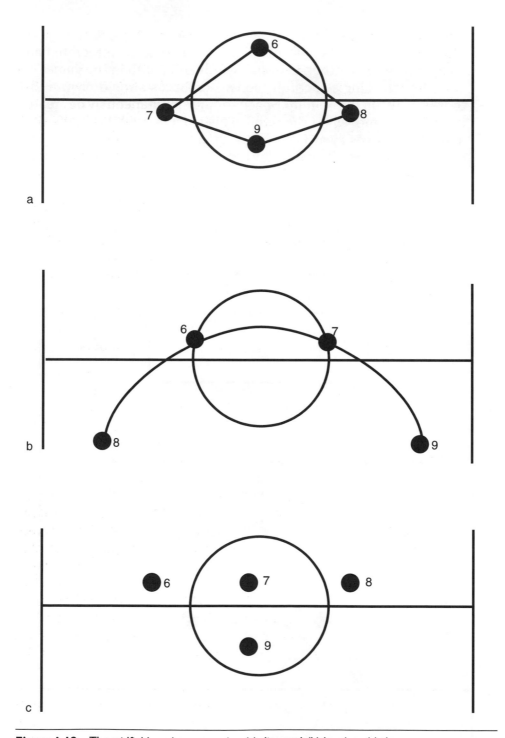

**Figure 1.12** The midfield can be arranged as (a) diamond, (b) bowl, or (c) three-one arrangement.

Between the two of them, they should know when to move forward and when they should hold back.

Both central defenders should be in supporting positions during the buildup of play. If a libero is part of the formation, this player should actively take part in the buildup.

Select the midfield formation to promote offensive support from the fullbacks and to utilize the qualities of the midfielders. The formation should create safe consolidation play as the basis of dynamic penetrating play. Aside from the options for combinations, the midfielders should also be ready to receive the ball in the attacking zone and to pick up second balls outside the penalty area. Support for the attackers is also vital, using, for example, diagonal runs into the opposition's defensive zone. The two attackers should move with full awareness of each other's positions. If they position themselves around the center of defense, they attract at least two defenders and, at the same time, they are in a position to make diagonal runs out toward the wings, one at a time. By taking up positions a long way from each other, they can create space for forward-breaking midfielders, and they can set in motion a blind-side run.

## Defending

Defensively, 4-4-2 is usually organized by zonal marking, which assures appropriate cover of all areas on the team's own half of the pitch.

The two attackers should work as a pair and either cover the opposition's buildup on one of the side areas or position themselves centrally and apply pressure to a defender to whom the ball may be played. By the choice of midfield formation, the team can invite the opposition to take up particular directions of play. If the four players form, for example, a bowl shape, this invites the opposition to play through the middle, while the wings are conversely closed off. If the four midfielders make a diamond shape, the position of the offensive midfielder, in relation to the ball and his two attacking teammates, dictates the opposition's buildup of play. A well-organized midfield will be an advantage in the transition from defense to attack because it will generally be easy to find a quick passing option on winning the ball.

With defensive cooperation between defense and midfield, the team can use the pressure game. The defense can be organized with a sweeper or a libero. A "flat back" defense, where the four players are in a line, calls for a cautious goalkeeper, who can, on occasion, also fulfill the role of sweeper. The effectiveness of the defensive unit depends on the players' ability to move across and maintain balance according to the changing defensive situations.

## How Brazil Played 4-4-2 During the 1994 World Cup

### Starting Formation

The Brazilian world champions of 1994 played in a 4-4-2 formation, and the team's skill showed off the qualities of the system. In the final, the team lined up as shown in figure 1.13.

### Attacking

The offensive force in the buildup centered on the wings. The two fullbacks created great width for the buildup. When one of the central defenders, Santos, took an active part in the early buildup combinations, the opposition's strikers were pushed onto one of the wings. This created space on the opposite side, where the other fullback

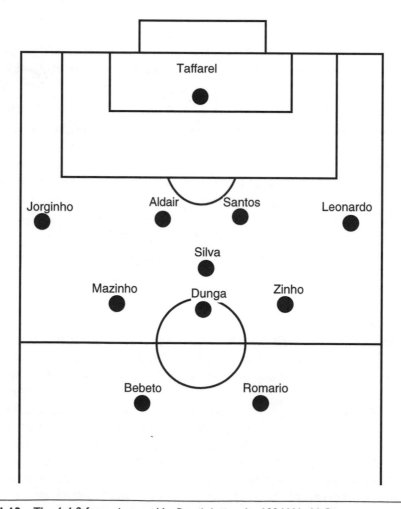

**Figure 1.13**   The 4-4-2 formation used by Brazil during the 1994 World Cup.

During the 1994 World Cup, the Brazilian midfield player Dunga played an important role when the ball was brought through the center midfield.

could be played as he ran to the ball. The Brazilian team put a lot of effort into penetration from the wings, and a fullback often participated in combination play farther up the pitch, so that a cross could come in from the wing. Apart from the constant drives by fullbacks toward the goal line, there were also diagonal runs inside and out toward the wings from one of the strikers—Bebeto in particular. In this way, the team constantly tried to create both depth and width in the game. At the same time, the Brazilian players' high technical level was utilized. Play was very narrow and fast (first-time passes), with players at full pace bringing the ball forward from the back and inviting a combination leading to a breakthrough.

## Defending

The defensive unit was organized with two central defenders who supported each other. In front of them, Mauro Silva, as the defensive midfield player, was a vital component in the immovable center of defense. The Brazilian one-three midfield formation with the chosen players, together with the two central defenders, gave the team a physically strong backbone.

Brazil has traditionally played very deep defensively, and the 1994 world champions did not alter this. After an explosive attack, the players moved slowly back home toward their own half of the pitch and organized themselves in their areas. They tried to cover the player with the ball without attempting to win it, and only when the opponent made a weak pass did the actual phase of regaining possession begin. The attempts at winning the ball occurred, as a rule, not through body tackles, but chiefly by nudging the ball away from the opponent.

## *Sample Training Session Using 4-4-2*

We have provided an example of how the coach can train a team playing 4-4-2 in one of the main characteristics of the system, that of width in the buildup in order to utilize the fullbacks. See figure 1.14.

### Pitch

Three-quarter pitch with one full-size goal.

### Players

Seven black and three white players, plus one goalkeeper.

### Organization

Fixed pattern followed by normal play.

### Description

The black team has a set playing pattern following winning the ball or restarting play. The central defender (number 3) plays the offensive midfield player (number 8), who plays the nearest attacker (number 10) who should offer himself. He passes with one touch only back to 6, who opens the game up by playing 2, the forward running fullback, on the wing. The fullback should come forward to cross. When the fullback receives the ball, play is without restrictions. The practice can be varied by allowing a pass from 8 to 9 or 10, thus varying from which side the attack comes.

The playing pattern is carried out at first at a controlled tempo, and then at normal speed.

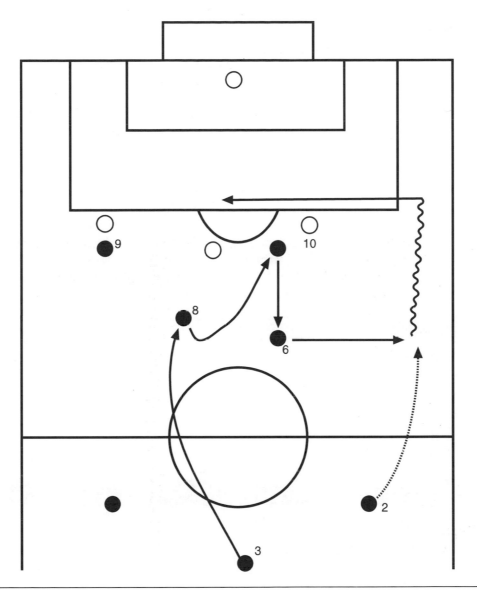

**Figure 1.14**   4-4-2 training session.

## Conditions

When the white team has the ball, the two attackers may not try to win it. Number 3 may not cross the halfway line. When the black team wins the ball, it should be played back to number 3.

## Scoring

The attacking team scores in the big goal, and the defenders score by passing to the goalkeeper.

## Variations

1.  Number 3 may play directly to 9 or 10.
2.  Other players can join in the set pattern.

## Coaching Points

The game is a standard buildup form that focuses on how width in a game can be utilized in a 4-4-2 system by creating options for using the fullbacks down the wings. Playing up into the middle of the pitch in the first phase causes the opposition's midfield to be grouped centrally, and this creates more space at the sides. The fullbacks should be patient and wait until 8 has control of the ball before breaking forward. Number 8 should look for a free space when 3 has a chance to play the ball forward. The other midfielders should try to create space for 8. When 8 receives the pass from 3, the two attackers should be prepared to break toward 8, and 6 should take up a position where he can receive a backpass from 9 or 10.

## Keywords

Group the midfield centrally • Be patient with the forward run • Come forward to cross

# The 3-5-2 System

## Starting Formation

Three players in defense, five midfielders, two attackers, and a goal-keeper (see figure 1.7, page 9).

## Organization

The defensive unit is organized with two players who mark the opposition's attackers (markers) and a sweeper. The midfield unit consists of two wingbacks and three central midfielders, who can organize themselves either in a line or with a defensive or an offensive midfield player (see figure 1.15). The two attackers are positioned well up the pitch and often function as a central and a floating striker.

## Attacking

In the buildup of attacking play, the sweeper should normally make himself available for goalkeeper distribution. Using their positions,

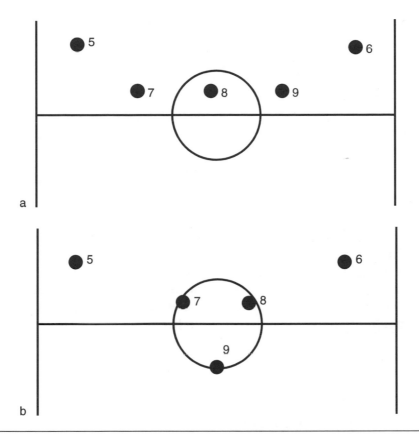

**Figure 1.15**   The five midfield players can arrange themselves (a) in a line or (b) with an offensive midfield player.

the two markers create space for the sweeper's forward pass and can also become passing options when their opponents try to pressure the player with the ball. A marker who wins the ball should usually pass it on quickly, to avoid the ball being won back in a dangerous area. It should either be played back to the goalkeeper or libero, or deep into the opposition's half.

The two wingbacks should ensure width in the game, and their areas of functioning are in the 10-meter corridors between the side-lines and the playing area. During the buildup, one of them should often move down toward the defensive zone, to be in a position to start a buildup on the other side. Many teams use a standard buildup, begun via one wingback who tries to push the buildup forward to the halfway line. If the wingback is challenged, the ball is played back and then swiftly over to the other side, where a free space has been created for the other wingback.

The most important aspects of the wingback's attacking role are seeking constantly to exploit the corridor area, so the opposition shifts defensive organization to one side; and in the breakthrough phase, coming up to the goal line and making a cross. A well-developed bit of teamwork with another midfielder, say, via overlap, can create effective breakthrough opportunities. Overlaps can also work with an attacker. The attackers should position themselves centrally in the center area and make diagonal runs out toward the sidelines according to the area where the buildup is based.

In the three defenders' marking roles, it is essential that the two markers never compromise in their defense. They should be close to their direct opponents, who are not permitted the space to turn when the ball is played to them. In most situations, markers should concentrate on winning the ball immediately. With the sweeper behind them, the markers can allow themselves to concentrate on winning the ball.

The system's value is the central defensive cover in front of the goal and the exploitation of a strengthened midfield area with regard to both attack and defense. At the same time, the system's weakness lies in the restricted defense, which often gives the opposition great opportunities to utilize the width in the defensive zone.

## How Barcelona Played 3-5-2 in 1994

### Starting Formation

The team appeared as shown in figure 1.16.

### Attacking

Barcelona's style of play during the 1994 season was extremely offensive in character—a constant search for finishing opportunities. The pervasive attacking principle was to pass deep and never straight across. The players carried out this idea by grouping themselves in almost a triangular arrangement pointing up the pitch (see figure 1.17). They consciously played the ball between the opposition's midfielders. In the buildup from the defensive unit, they made deep penetrating passes beyond the opposition's four midfielders to other team members who, through diagonal runs, brought themselves into positions to receive the ball. In the attacking zone, individual players exploited their dribbling talents—and breaks in the gaps behind the defense. To create gaps, the team often used Romario's "magnet" effect, where, by moving away from the forward line, he took a defender with him. By doing this, he created free space that was either utilized by the player himself, with his fantastic ability to change speed, or by his teammates who would break inside. Michael Laudrup's value to the team was his interaction with Romario and Stoichkov, who, in particular, exploited his speed effectively in combination play.

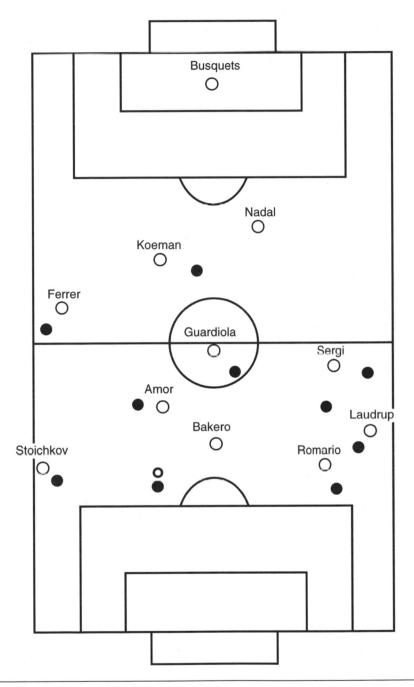

**Figure 1.16**    Barcelona's 3-5-2 formation in 1994.

## Defending

Even if Barcelona did not overemphasize the importance of defense,
there were clearly rehearsed routines in the team's defensive play.
The three-man unit consisted of two markers, Ferrer and Nadal, who

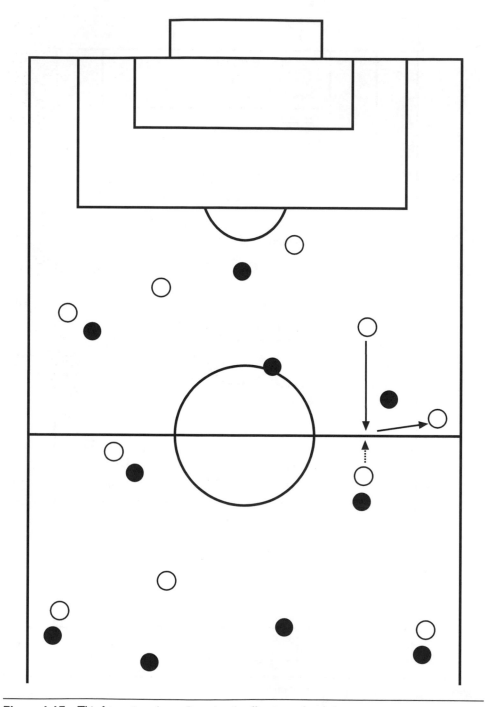

**Figure 1.17** This formation shows Barcelona's offensive style of play.

Michael Laudrup played a central role in Barcelona's penetration play during the early 1990s.

supported each other's strengths and weaknesses: Ferrer ruled the right defensive wing, was a master of close shielding, and was fast in one-on-one situations; Nadal covered the central midfield zone using his heading strength and good assessment skills as a basis. Between the two markers was Koeman—sometimes ahead of them, and occasionally, more traditionally, behind them. Koeman's defensive play was dependent on Guardiola, the defensive midfielder. If Guardiola did not cover the area in front of the box's edge, Koeman would move forward to close the gap. If Koeman went forward, Guardiola took charge behind him. Taken as a whole, there was a marked forward movement in the defensive play. The defenders rarely moved back down the pitch, which created less space for opponents. They had great belief in their own defensive ability.

On the left-hand side, the wingback Sergi possessed qualities similar to Ferrer's and could at times take over man marking for one of the others, if the need presented itself. The midfield's organization was usually looking toward the right (see figure 1.16). This organization was dictated in the first phase by Bakero in accordance with his position alongside Guardiola, who constantly backed him up behind the front of midfield. By maintaining the width in the five-man midfield, they forced the opposition to play through the center, where the three strongest markers, Guardiola, Bakero, and Amor, were positioned.

## Sample Training Session Using 3-5-2

Here we provide an example of how the coach can train a team using the 3-5-2 formation in one of the system's main characteristics, that of penetrating runs from midfield. See figure 1.18.

### Pitch

About three-quarter pitch, about 40 meters wide, with three zones (one to three), and one full-size goal.

### Players

Thirteen—eight black and five white players, one of whom is a goalkeeper.

### Organization

Three (black) versus one (white) in the defensive zone (1); three (black) versus one (white) in the midfield zone (2); and two-on-two in the attacking zone (3).

### Description

Normal play. The game starts on defense, and the ball should be passed forward to the two attackers in the attacking zone. The attackers can either control the ball for their own forward play or lay it off to the midfielder following them.

### Conditions

The players in the defensive and attacking zones may not leave their areas.

### Scoring

Score as normal for the black team. The white team scores either by winning the ball in the defensive zone or by playing its one attacker, who controls the ball.

### Variations

1. The number of white players increases in the defensive and attacking zones.

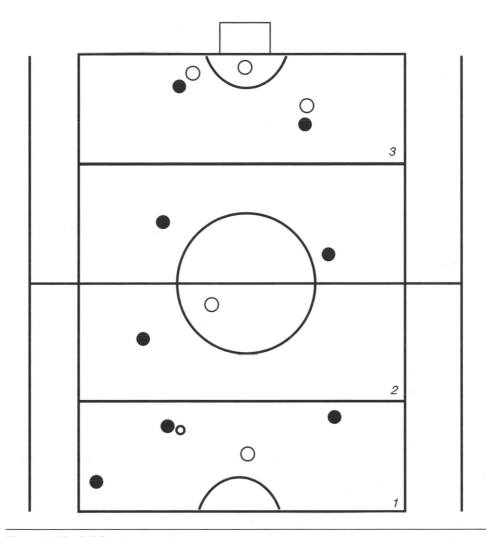

**Figure 1.18**  3-5-2 training session.

2. The number of players increases correspondingly in the defensive and attacking zones while the pitch is widened.

3. In the midfield zone, the game is five versus four, and in the attacking zone, it's two versus three on a pitch of normal width.

**Coaching Points**

The training focuses on how to exploit offensive strength through the crowded midfield area, especially with forward runs from midfield. This means that a midfielder ought to be able to find the right moment to make a forward run or a pass up to the attackers. The midfielders often stay behind the attackers as supporting players, but it is also vital simply to break away from the forward line. This practice lends itself to the assessment and training of the timing and options for moves between the midfield and attacking units.

## Keywords

Decoy run • Forward play • Push up

# The 3-4-3 System

### Starting Formation

Three players in the defensive unit, four midfielders, and three attackers (see figure 1.19). The division of the players into the three units obviously sets the scene for a style of play where the main part of the game will take place in the opposition's half of the field.

### Organization

The few players on defense are positioned in accordance with the fact that the opposition often plays with one or two attackers. No one wants four players to be tied up with only two opponents, and it is not unusual to see the best teams playing with only two at the back if the opposition is only playing one striker. The three attackers are positioned in such a way that width is a natural feature of the attacking play.

### Attacking

The attackers should not trap themselves by getting too close to the opposition's defenders. The two wingers should move back down the pitch to become available. This normally occurs when play is on the opposite side of the pitch. The two wingers are often fast, and by moving back down the pitch for a short distance on receiving the ball, they can more easily turn away from the defenders and reach a high speed before the challenge. The system is based on well-developed teamwork between the outer midfield players and wingers, and between the central attacker and the rest of midfield.

### Defending

As a rule, the three on defense play with zonal marking, but when the opposition, who is controlling play, encroaches over the halfway line, the closest defender should challenge the potential attacker who is in the relevant area. Defenders maintain the switch to man-to-man

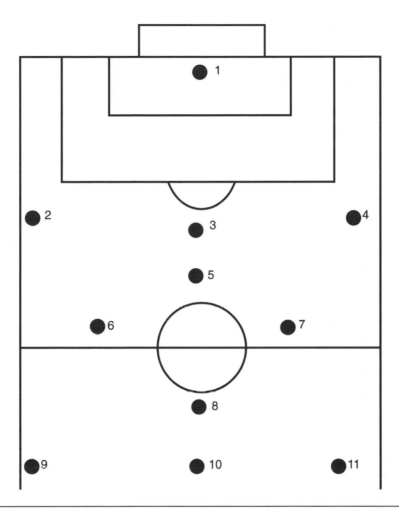

**Figure 1.19**   The 3-4-3 formation.

marking until the situation is cleared. It is commonly the right and left backs who undertake the man-to-man marking, while the third player functions as a sweeper. If the attacker is in the central area, number 3 will mark this player, and either 5 or one of the wide backs will act in support.

The organization of the midfield is crucial in giving confidence to the few players on defense. At the commencement of play, number 5 is a free player and could be classified as a libero who is pushing forward. Number 5 operates defensively according to the situation; this is usually as the defensive midfield player, but also as the player who gets right back if it looks as if the opposition is about to break through on one of the wings. The four midfielders should cover the open space in the midfield area. When the opposition has the ball and is in the process of a buildup, players consciously try to centralize the game in this area. The players' positions form a diamond, but a tight diamond. This means that the area along the sides of the defensive half of the pitch should normally be covered by the two wingers. The central attacker should remain central in both the offensive and defensive phases.

## How Ajax Played 3-4-3 in 1995

### Starting Formation

The Champions League winners of 1995 started as shown in figure 1.20. The essence of Ajax's style is that every player can do the work of another, and do it with so much technical reserve and tactical insight that he does not at any moment appear to be out of position.

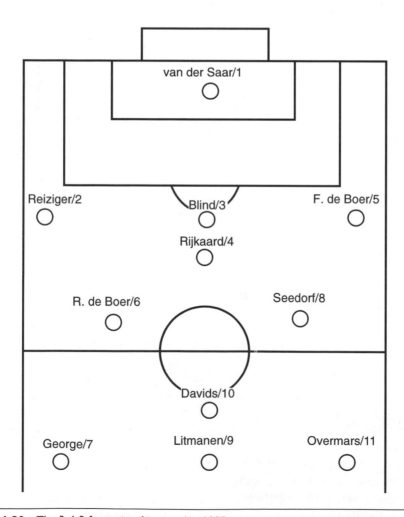

**Figure 1.20**   The 3-4-3 formation Ajax used in 1995.

A definite aim is for any player to be able to play three positions within his line in the formation. That is to say, for example, that Ronald de Boer, starting from his right midfield position, can play right back and right wing.

## Attacking

The three attackers are positioned with two traditional wingers and one center forward. This spreads out the opposition's defense and keeps it very deep. That, in turn, means the attackers can more easily make themselves playable by breaking toward the player with the ball or positioning themselves along the sidelines. One of the main tasks of the two wingers, due to their speed, is to try to penetrate the opposition's defense. They work closely with the wide midfielders and often switch positions so that, on receiving the ball, the winger drops off, while his colleague breaks forward into the wing area. The central attacker, Litmanen, often moves back down the pitch to receive passes from the units behind him, and the ball is played directly to him. He tends to take one of the central defenders with him, and by controlling and holding the ball with his side turned to his opponent, he keeps the attention of the defense. While this is happening, other members of the team get into good positions, either for combination play or to find free spaces behind the marking defender.

By playing wide in the buildup, the defensive unit becomes a vital link in switching sides. In consolidation, play alternates between depth and width, and passes directly to the center forward. At times, the style can be reminiscent of the game played along defensive lines in team handball.

## Defending

Ajax begins its defense in the center of the opposition's midfield. Two players are vital to the system's strength in both attack and defense, namely Rijkaard (4), who can position himself both ahead of and behind Blind; and Litmanen (10), who can charge right forward into attack or move back into the midfield. They are both positioned on a line running lengthwise down the center of the pitch but can be moved forward depending on the tactical requirements.

The two wingers work using defensive runs and blocking the opposition's two fullbacks along the wings. If a fullback still gets through, the winger remains forward, forcing one of the other defenders to move correspondingly.

The defensive unit plays in a line, usually with a sweeper in front of the defense. This means that the defenders need to have great confidence in their individual experience and ability to successfully negotiate one-on-one situations.

## Sample Training Session Using 3-4-3

Here we have provided an example of how the coach can train a team using 3-4-3 in one of the system's main characteristics, that of wing play. See figure 1.21.

### Pitch

Pitch with three zones (one to three) and a full-size goal.

### Players

Fifteen—eight black and seven white, one of whom is a goalkeeper.

### Organization

The black team outnumbers the white in zones one and three (three versus two).

### Description

Normal play. Black number 4 receives a goal kick from the white goalkeeper, then plays the ball into either zone one or zone three. The three black players, numbers 5, 7, and 11, should play themselves forward for a cross or a pass to the opposite zone, possibly via zone

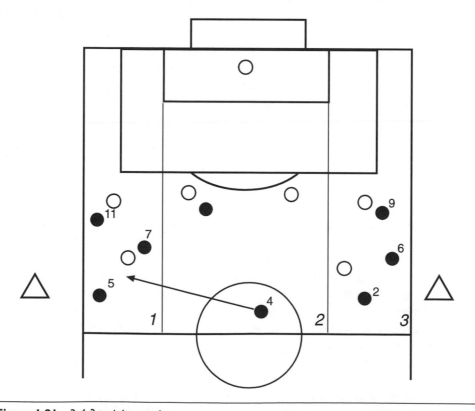

**Figure 1.21**   3-4-3 training session.

two. When the cross comes in, there is no zonal limitation, but 5, 7, or 11 should attempt a finish within two deliveries and immediately following any return balls. The players in zones one and three should decide upon the patterns of attack and practice them systematically. For example, 5 plays to 11, who makes a decoy run, while 7 has moved into a position to receive the ball. Number 11 plays the ball back to 5, who plays the ball deep to 7.

### Conditions

The black team's players may not leave their respective zones.

### Scoring

As normal for the black team. If the white team wins the ball, or when the goalkeeper has possession of the ball, the team may score by either number 2 or number 5 receiving and controlling a pass 40 meters from the goal line, on the other side of a cone marker. Of the black team players, only 9 or 11 may run back and try to prevent 2 and 5 from receiving the ball.

### Coaching Points

The game focuses on utilizing the two wingers in attack and defense. From an attacking point of view, it is important that the players rehearse several attacking patterns, which can create variations in play down the wings and will ensure many crosses behind the defense. The two wingers should also be encouraged to attempt to penetrate the defense, with their teammates behind in support.

On defense, decisive roles in the system are the two wingers' abilities to close off the wings, so the opposition's fullbacks and midfield players do not have time or space for buildup and consolidation in this area. Scoring chances for the white team emphasize the need for the two wingers to make backward runs.

## Keywords

Penetration through the wings • Quick finishes • Close down the opposition's fullback

# CHAPTER 2

# Styles of Play

A style of play is the characteristic way in which a team uses a system of play. Selecting a style of play should take into account the playing qualities a team possesses. Above all, the coach should ask the following: "To what type of soccer do the playing qualities at my disposal immediately offer themselves? Is there great offensive potential, or is it a matter of more all-around play? How do I assess the four basic areas of the players: their physical capacity, technical foundation, tactical level, and psychological balance?"

The coach should match up and adapt these considerations when selecting the team's system of play, so that all resources are utilized optimally (see chapter 3). This also brings out a completely individual approach to the game—a way of playing for each individual team—but there is some common ground when the coach assesses different styles of play. This applies particularly to the choice between offensive and defensive play.

## Attacking Styles

The following descriptions of styles of play refer to international soccer, because it is here that the main components of a style become most obvious.

### Systematic Buildup of Play

This style is characterized by a meticulous buildup consisting of many passes between defense and midfield. Another term is "possession soccer," where a team "owns" the ball and tries to keep possession of it. The idea is to try to push many players forward and then establish the game in the last third of the pitch. The team keeps the ball patiently during attempts to create an opening until it can make a breakthrough. At times, the play around the opposition's defensive unit can be reminiscent of passing play in team handball. However, the opening is also created through risky play. Normally, any team with good technical players can use this style.

## Direct Play

In contrast to possession soccer, direct play means that a team consciously plays the ball quickly forward to the opposition's third and tries to finish quickly.

An important context is that the opposition's defense is often somewhat disorganized at the moment the ball is regained—something this style seeks to exploit. If a team exclusively knocks the ball up the pitch, it is described as "kick and rush" soccer.

## Counterattacking Play

By consciously allowing the opposition to come well up the pitch, a team creates conditions for establishing counterattacking play. This means a fast, direct counterattack with few players, set in motion when the ball is won, followed by a quick pass played over many opponents. In the instant of passing, one or two players should rush forward to support the player who receives the ball in plenty of space.

## Total Soccer

The term total soccer was first used to refer to the Dutch team's style of play at the 1974 World Cup. Total soccer is a style of play where the players, stretched very widely, switch positions during the buildup play. A quasi rotational system between midfield and attack ensures that the opposition's marking is more difficult, especially if the opposition is playing with man-marking.

The Dutch 1988 European Championship winners, with Gullit, van Basten, Rijkaard and Koeman, continued the ideas of total soccer.

# Defensive Styles

Here we describe defensive styles of play used internationally: collective defensive style, low-pressure style, and pressure play.

## Collective Defensive Style—Block Defending

The block style is based on a 4-4-2 system with a flat-back four, organized using consistent zonal marking on the defensive half of the pitch. The style is recognizable by its strong collective responsibility in marking, which ought to ensure that no large gaps appear between the players' areas of responsibility. In defensive play, visualize a thread of elastic between the players; "see" the way it pulls them according to the center of play. The synchronized patterns of movements are carried out with good communication between the players.

## Low-Pressure Style—Team Handball

When a team, on losing the ball or finishing on goal, consciously moves back down its own half of the pitch, this is called the low-pressure style. Out on the pitch, we often see teams begin a definite defensive effort only when the ball passes the halfway line. In order to hinder the opposition's chances of finishing, the team introduces a two-unit style of marking close to its own penalty area and extending across the width of the pitch. This style of marking is reminiscent of team handball marking on the three-meter line.

## Pressure Play

Pressure play is an offensive style of defense where the team tries to win the ball as quickly and close to the opposition's goal as possible. It requires speedy pressure on the player with the ball and a simultaneous push up by other members of the team in the area. In order to support the pressure in the midfield area, a player, say a libero, will normally get position in front of the defense. Offside is often played.

# National Characteristics

National teams display unique characteristics resulting from specific players' talents combined with the dynamics of the team and coach and sometimes relating to the country's culture. Certain games and championships have clearly exemplified these characteristics.

## The Latin Style

Characteristic of most top Italian and Spanish teams is their use of a meticulous and patient buildup, called the Latin style. This means that many passes are exchanged between defense and midfield in order to move lots of players forward. The idea is to center play in the opposition's half of the pitch. Opponents often allow this buildup so they can create the conditions for a counterattack.

The Italian soccer culture also emphasizes "la bella figura"—the beautiful handling of the ball, so that elegant combination play becomes naturally sought-after. The number 10, the offensive midfield player, is the decisive player when the center of play is first established. It is this individual who is expected to set the scene for a breakthrough.

# The British Style

The well-known British style of play has its foundations in the basic characteristics of the British worker culture from the end of the 1880s right up to the mid-1960s. Keywords are collectivity, manliness, and tradition. The game values fighting qualities and the direct challenge. The most widely used expression in British soccer, therefore, is: "Put it in the box," that is, the direct route to goal (the penalty area). The style of play is recognizable by the use of simple methods and full speed ahead.

During the 1980s, the director of coaching for the English Football (Soccer) Association, Charles Hughes, outlined his recipe for what he called the Winning Formula. The book of the same name is a critique of the possession style. Adherents of the possession style of play advocate the worth of being able to move opponents away from their appropriate positions and, by indirect combination play, utilizing the openings that arise. In contrast to this, Hughes advocates that when the ball is won, it should be played forward with the aim of finishing within five subsequent deliveries.

The understanding of the direct style of play is based on statistics encompassing 109 elite-level matches (including Liverpool, World Cup, and European Championship matches). The material shows that 87 percent of all goals are scored following an attack consisting of five or fewer deliveries. Also, a team has its best chance of success when it wins the ball in the opposition's defensive zone. More than 52 percent of all goals are scored in attacks originating in the team's own attacking zone.

This also means that defensive play starts in winning the ball as close to the opposition's goal as possible. A team is most vulnerable in that instant when the ball is lost. Therefore, the defender's units should be close together, because simply by remaining compact they can pressure the player with the ball, so the ball handler cannot play forward. There will be several players in the vicinity of the ball, and they can help apply pressure.

When pressuring players win the ball, they should put it into the attacking zone as quickly and directly as possible. Play should therefore consist of long passes forward. The passer should either put the ball behind the opposition's defense or play it directly to a teammate. To exploit the long pass, it is important that many players move forward quickly, either to receive the pass in a free area or as supporting players for a teammate who has received the ball and is facing away from the opposition's goal. The game in the attacking zone is primarily recognizable by the use of dribbling and of crosses from the wings.

People with knowledge of statistics, however, do not agree with these conclusions. During the 1986 World Cup, a comparison was made of the different playing styles of the teams that reached the semifinals and teams that did not succeed. The results demonstrated a difference regarding the

The British and Norwegian styles of play are characterized by the long ball, which is played forward to the strikers. This photograph shows the British player Sheringham during the 1996 European Championships.

number of touches on the ball. The semifinals teams, the successful ones, had 5.59 touches per possession of the ball, while the other teams, the unsuccessful ones, had 5.22 touches. This is an acknowledgment that the successful teams played more positional play than the others.

Taking into consideration the fact that teams often exchanged few passes within the team and, thus, that the probability of scoring after only a few passes was greater, no connection was found between the number of passes and the chance of scoring.

## The Norwegian Style—The Computer Style

Inspired by the ideas on which "direct play" is based, the Norwegian national team developed its own style of play. Norway qualified for the final stages of the 1994 World Cup with eye-opening victories over, among others, Holland and England; but the team progressed no farther than the three introductory group matches. The Norwegian style of play has, however, caused a stir, not least because it was based upon systematic observations and statistical materials from international matches.

The style of play is based on a 4-5-1 formation, and its vital elements consist of a tight defensive organization and a standardized attacking style. The team is organized according to zonal marking, both in the back and midfield units. It is here, among other places, that the team's playing style differs from that of other teams. The five midfielders are almost in a straight line, and each has an area to cover in the middle of the pitch. The defensive work takes place as a kind of knock-on effect. The nearest midfielder moves forward and pressures the opposition player in posses-sion of the ball. When the player with the ball either leaves that area or plays the ball out to the side, the pressuring midfielder should move quick as lightning back in line, and the next midfield player should move forward and create pressure (see figure 2.1). The quick turn back to the line is a crucial point in the effectiveness of the play because, in a short instant, an empty space is created behind the pressuring player. Observations of other teams show that when a player has been forward to pressure an opponent, he often remains forward once the player with the ball has vacated the area.

Aside from the aggressive pressure on the player with the ball, the team members gather in the vicinity of the ball, which means that the distance between the five midfielders is relatively small. If the opposition's buildup play takes place down one of the wings, the unit pushes across.

The long pass is another decisive element in the Norwegian style. It is a set, rehearsed pattern when the opposition's defensive arrangement is balanced. Normally, a fullback passes the long ball diagonally to Jostein Flo—tall and strong in the air. The midfielders simultaneously break forward around Flo, so as to be in the area where they can pick up or receive the ball, and the Norwegian starts the attacking play. The striker should be

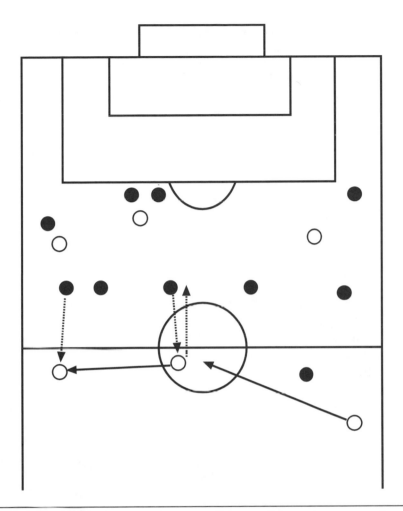

**Figure 2.1** In the Norwegian style of play, the midfielders move forward to pressure the opponent with the ball.

prepared to move inside the area behind the defense if the ball is flicked or headed on, and the remaining midfielders act according to the outcome of the duel for the ball. The long pass also means that the ball should quickly be regained high up the pitch if the opposition wins this duel.

The idea of quickly regaining possession and playing the ball on constitutes the third element in the Norwegian style of play. A team tries to get a "head start" when the opposition has lost the ball. This requires players to have something of a nose for those situations that create ball-winning opportunities—and also to play with a certain degree of flair. It can be profitable for a team to quickly create a situation where it outnumbers the opponent, thereby causing the opposition to be unbalanced from the start of the attack. As the Norwegians put it, in this phase, the players should try aggressively to penetrate the opposition.

## The South American Style (Futebol Bailado)

The Brazilian style of play is characterized by its unpredictable switches from lazy, easy, nonchalant handling of the ball at a walking pace to short-lived explosions of dynamic, angled, one-touch passes into the penalty area. In the penetration phase itself, many features are attempted with artistic proficiency.

The varied rhythm changes, combined with a languid manner of handling the ball, have never before been put into the context of a team tactical strategy, but have been of an impulsive nature. This has meant, among other things, that in the larger tournaments, Brazilian teams have not always reached the heights the team's flair in the introductory matches promised. However, the 1994 World Cup team and 1994 World Champion was basically defensive in character and sported a European-inspired style of defense. This seems to have provided a better basis for the superior qualities of the Brazilian players, and through this they maintained the free development of the players within a tighter organization than the very vague limits of earlier days.

Other Latin American soccer-playing nations demonstrate a variation of the Brazilian style, the telephone box style. Using a slow buildup in attack, a team has one or two players who, on the opposition's half of the pitch, consciously hold the ball and seek challenges from opponents. When two or three opponents have been lured out, the ball is dribbled out of the tight

Speedy Romario was repeatedly in a position to break free of the opposition during the 1994 World Cup.

area (the telephone box) and passed, creating a chance. By luring the opponents toward them, the players also attempt to create superiority of numbers in other areas of the pitch. A cheeky but fascinating tactic.

## The African Style

African soccer has finally reached the world stage. During the past 20 years, some African players have found their way into the professional leagues of Europe, but, first with Cameroon and more recently following Nigeria's unexpected World Cup performances, there has been a lot of talk of a future "great" area of the soccer world. The general opinion hitherto had been that African soccer possessed clever technicians and creative players, but that it was tactically unschooled. The tactical understanding has grown, and an important factor in the increased observation and successful performances is that several of the players now have European experience, which they use to influence the domestic players.

The African style is unorthodox, by European standards, with regard to the way the players use their bodies. In many players, it is often an enormous physical resource which, together with good rhythm, gives them the edge in one-on-one situations. Poor shooting and the nerve or will to finish are still the Africans' greatest weaknesses.

The Nigerian Olympic champions, with their combination of physical strength, well-developed technique, and tactical cunning, demonstrated that African soccer can be an international force.

# CHAPTER 3

# Team Tactics: Determination and Adjustment

*Team tactics* means finding the best ways to use basic tactical principles and deciding which actions will give the best attacking and defensive options. The individual team's tactics should be laid out according to both a long-term objective and the desire to win the next match.

## Choice

A good soccer team is well organized. This is one of the key factors in modern soccer, equal to a well-planned structure and clear role expectation and distribution.

In the game of soccer, players are organized into systems of play, as described both historically and currently in the previous chapters. Characteristically, a championship team organized in a new way or variation becomes a school for the styles of play of countless other teams. This is the copycat effect. Another influence can be the perspective effect, where a coach weighs possible changes or adjustments to the team's current system and way of playing. The massive media coverage of both national and international soccer gives rise to constant new impulses. These can be both inspiring and confusing, so an important element in the coach's role is knowing what the basics are when working with the organization and ongoing development of the team.

A coach has certain ideas about the way soccer should be played and how the team should play it. On the other hand, the coach quickly discovers how difficult it is to sell these ideals to the players—not just because of their abilities, but also because of time limitations.

The development of organization is a constant tug-of-war between what the coach ideally wants and what there is a real chance of achieving. There are two main ways to develop a system. One takes the condition of the players as a basis. The other prioritizes a prerehearsed system, and players who can simply adapt to the system are brought in or developed. Ajax is an example of the latter concept, while a national team's system of play, say, the Brazilian World Cup team of 1994, must to a great extent take into consideration the qualities the team possesses.

For both viewpoints, however, there is one common thread. The players' ways of completing individual playing situations are what decides the team's success. Players, not systems, win matches.

# The Coach's Role Before the Match

Decisions about which tactical strong points to incorporate into the team's style of play during a match are based on knowledge of

- the team's qualities,
- the opposition's style of play, and
- specific conditions.

## The Team's Qualities

Knowledge of the capacity of one's own players is the decisive factor when working out team tactics. The coach should be familiar with the technical levels of the players, their physical capacities, and their minds. Team tactics can, almost without exception, work only if they are laid out using this kind of analysis. It is unfortunate when the coach's ambitious tactical plans are completely out of proportion to the condition of the players.

Soccer tactics are readily written down and can appear misleadingly easy, but performing them requires many training sessions. There are no shortcuts. It is particularly important that the coach evaluate the team's strong points with reference to tactics.

## Knowledge of the Opposition

At elite levels, a coach often has in-depth knowledge of opposing teams. This is all part of good preparation while deciding upon team tactics. The coach should, however, be cautious when assessing the information. It is not necessary to take into account everything the opposing team has done in recent matches or to weigh all details when considering tactics. The important thing is to be able to pinpoint the factors that are important for strengthening the coach's own team's attacking and defensive options. As a basis for observing an opposing team, table 3.1 (on page 52), by the former Danish national coach, Sepp Piontek, is very illuminating.

## Specific Conditions

Specific conditions can be both internal and external in character. Internal conditions can be, say, regarding the match's importance relative to league position. If the team has undergone substantial changes in setup due, for example, to injury, this can have a great impact on tactics and on how far the team can be pushed. External conditions include such matters as the state of the pitch (dry or wet) or the angle of the sun in the first and second halves relative to the goalkeeper.

## Team Feedback

It is the players who have to live with tactical decisions. Therefore, it's important that decisions are made corresponding to the knowledge at hand and are as widely supported as possible.

Responsibility for such decisions rises proportionally with the influence the players have on the process. Their influence will ensure that the team's tactical goals appear realistic and attainable to them. The introduction of a tactic will normally be the coach's consideration, but a dialogue afterward will promote the possibility of the tactic being used.

The coach should introduce and clarify a tactic for a coming match as early as possible—for example, on Monday if the game is on Saturday or Sunday. This allows for training in the individual factors to be considered for the next match. A German ex-national coach's saying hits the nail on the head here: "After the match is before the match."

# The Coach's Role During the Match

When the team runs onto the pitch, it is with confidence both of the coach and the players that they are employing the correct tactic. A tactic is, however, not infallible, and during the course of two 45-minute halves— and between them—it can be adjusted or changed. This applies particularly

## Table 3.1   Observation of Opposition During a Match

**System**

| | |
|---|---|
| ❑ 4-3-3 | ❑ 4-4-2 |
| ❑ 5-3-2 | ❑ offensive or defensive focus |
| ❑ zonal marking | |
| ❑ man-marking | |

**Style of play**

| | |
|---|---|
| ❑ technical or fighting | ❑ normal or aggressive |
| ❑ long or short passes | ❑ changes of tempo |

**Organization of defense**

| | |
|---|---|
| ❑ zonal marking | ❑ man-marking |
| ❑ tight or loose marking | ❑ support |
| ❑ division of labor | ❑ push up |
| ❑ offside | |

**Midfield play**

| | |
|---|---|
| ❑ division of labor | ❑ playmaker |

**Attacking play**

| | |
|---|---|
| ❑ play without the ball | ❑ play on the wings |
| ❑ stages of play | ❑ dribbling |
| ❑ overlap | ❑ finishing |
| ❑ defensive support | |

**Dead-ball situations**

| | |
|---|---|
| ❑ free kicks | ❑ corner kicks |
| ❑ walls | ❑ penalty kicks |
| ❑ throw-ins | |

**Physical capacity**

| | |
|---|---|
| ❑ first half | ❑ second half |

**Individual players**

| | |
|---|---|
| ❑ personalities | ❑ technicians |
| ❑ fighters | ❑ speed |
| ❑ heading | ❑ dribbling |
| ❑ passing | ❑ danger in front of goal |

**General impressions**

**Detailed impressions**

Morten Olsen demonstrated through his long international career the importance of an attacker to a team and coach.

to the halftime rest, when the coach can lay out alterations clearly for the players. That's normally a matter of making corrections in response to first-half events. If the prearranged tactic needs an important change, its consequences for the players involved should be described clearly. This also includes specific matters such as substitutions—or the discussion of possible substitutions. It is important to formulate second-half tactics from first-half experiences, and for the team to utilize its own strengths and the opposition's weaknesses. Likewise, it is natural to point the way individually.

Table 3.2, as an example of match observation from the dugout, is former Danish national coach Sepp Piontek's diagram, which is readily

## Table 3.2    Match Analysis Phases

**Home Team**

Implementation of tactics
↓
Assessment of form

❑ team

❑ individual player
↓
Strengths, weaknesses
↓
Tempo

❑ correct

❑ too slow
↓
Analysis of action

❑ attack

❑ defense

❑ midfield
↓
Half time/break

❑ sort out tactics

❑ keep tabs on opposition activity

❑ new programming
↓
Second Half
↓
Observation of result
↓
Substitution

❑ offensive

❑ defensive
↓
70-75 minutes

❑ improve the result

❑ tactical intervention

**Opposition**

Anticipated system
↓
Tactical aims

❑ offensive

❑ defensive

❑ strengths

❑ weaknesses
↓
Strengths, weaknesses
↓
Analysis of action
↓
Half time/break
↓
Second Half
↓
Tactical changes

❑ system

❑ position
↓
Substitution

available. It shows schematically the phases in the course of a match that the coach should always summarize and assess.

# The Captain's Role

The captain's role is central to the communication between players and the coach. It is through the captain that the coach can adjust the tactical layout. Even if, nowadays, the coach is allowed to give players tactical advice during the match, there will be many situations where oral instruction is impossible.

The coach can thus use sign language to communicate important attacking and defensive principles, such as width, crossover-run, and slowing the game down.

# CHAPTER 4

# Tactical Training

In soccer, we primarily know the principles of how to improve physical abilities and technical skills. There are, as yet, no clear guidelines as to the best way to train players' tactical skills and develop a group so that it becomes a strong unit, but through the learning process a team can strengthen skills and therefore grow as a group.

## The Tactical Learning Process

The aim of tactical training is to improve the individual's choice of action in different playing situations during the match. The individual player's tactical performance is based on tactical knowledge, tactical skills, and tactical abilities. In order for players to improve their tactical skills, they must have a solid understanding of these three issues.

Tactical knowledge encompasses knowledge in such areas as systems of play, basic rules of tactical play, and the rules of the game. Tactical skills are the actions which, through practice, a player carries out automatically following certain signals (stimuli). When the programmed response is insufficient in a specific situation, the player's tactical abilities come into play, and the player reasons out a chosen action.

### Analyzing Information

The cognitive processes during play are all based on the way information is taken on board and how it is analyzed. The process has four phases: perception, including attentional regulation; anticipation (assessment); choice of action; and feedback.

Good soccer players are quite perceptive; they understand and analyze the game situation very quickly. They have developed this ability through countless situation interpretations and experiences. Memory and experience are important prerequisites for gaining good anticipatory abilities. Having collected many experiences through time, a player has a good basis for reading the game. This element, however, is not just about having years of match background, but is also built up by training in specific tactical situations for a concentrated period of time. The coach must keep this in mind when improving tactical actions or incorporating new ones. If the coach values training in realistic game situations and concentrated work on certain tactical elements for short periods, the player will more rapidly gain the ability to decide on actions during a game. To reinforce choice of the correct actions, the coach must give players feedback about the results of the actions. A player can personally assess the appropriate action and add it to the memory bank. When a player practices a new or different tactical action pattern, it is also necessary for the coach to give quality feedback, which completes and enriches the player's own experience.

## Creating Tactical Knowledge and Insight

Tactical ability lies in the player's choice of action in a certain game situation. All tactical training must, therefore, take into account the fact that a player must make decisions during a game, thus creating the need to work on perception, evaluation, and choice of action. This learning process can be supported in several ways.

Coaches can create understanding and insight into tactical opportunities using theory sessions and practical training. A theoretical examination, which presents and investigates specific tactical skills or principles in depth, can often aid players' understanding of the principle's meaning and its context in the rest of the team's tactics. Coaches can highlight essential keywords using a blackboard and, perhaps, incorporating video clips, and the team may discuss ways players can use the desired action in a positive way.

It is practical training, however, that primarily establishes use. This training should consist of practices and games, placing varied and gradually increasing demands on players' perception skills. To work with an element, it is a good idea to start with a basic game or practice, which progressively becomes more advanced. Practices must finish by being so close to true game situations that there are many alternatives, from which optimal patterns of action arise. When introducing a new system, or when practicing with new players, the coach can start off with an 11-versus-4 game on a full-size pitch. A.C. Milan, among others, used this game for a short while with new players working to become accustomed to the team's system of play.

The coach should bring his tactical ideas onto the training pitch.

In the long term, the coach should prioritize a predetermined or connected set of tactical themes, so that there is a real chance to build up experiences and a kind of system in patterns of reaction. Learning or training, to create stable action patterns for specific game situations, will only take effect if it is part of a systematic, ongoing process.

The coach can use various instructional methods to enhance the learning process. These methods are described in the section, Methods of Training, in chapter 5. One factor common to all methods of instruction is communication between coach and players. Differences lie mostly in the varying opinions on the coach's role during instruction. As regards tactical training, the coach's guidance is vital. Games and practices must have a realistic aim; the coach must explain it and the players must understand it for learning to have any long-term effect.

Discussing tactical problems and solutions with the players is a good investment in time. Here, it is important to find those types of solutions that consider the individual player and to aim for a shared feeling of responsibility on the team. This kind of talk might also occur naturally in team meetings.

# Viewing Video Footage

Video recordings of the team's—or possibly other teams'—matches can be incorporated into tactical work. Surveying their own game action and having specific tactical situations pointed out to them enriches and influences players' tactical understanding. In the recording, coaches will generally observe tactical situations concerning their own team. To ensure the full attention of the players and, thus, the best effect on them, the coach must be thoroughly prepared as to what will be viewed, and for how long.

Time spent viewing videos must be limited for reasons of motivation, among others. German research notes that elite players are not interested in spending a lot of time watching video clips, which is to some extent explained by the fact that 90 percent of what they see there is irrelevant to them. There is often much rewinding and fast-forwarding in order to demonstrate—from the point of view of the coach—matters of interest; thus, the players lose attention and motivation.

For the coach's work, the match analysis is crucial. The table on page 54 outlines a way the coach can, during a match, assess the team's tactical play. Starting with the original ideas, combined with either mental or written notes of strengths and weaknesses in the team's performance during the game, the analysis provides a context for the next training session. This means it will be easier for the coach to locate the exact sections to show the players or use in planning a training session.

Dead-ball situations, unity between groups of players (runs, distance, passing angles, etc.), and analyses of individual performances are the most appropriate places to pay attention to tactical matters. Behind-the-goal filming of the goalkeeper's defense, for example, can start off an analysis. Through recorded sound and pictures, the goalkeeper can relive the performance or "experience" that of another player in the area. The goalkeeper and the coach may have quite different ideas of that game's work, and these recordings can act as a good basis for paying more attention to the goalkeeper's role. Players may also take the footage home with them and observe their own contributions themselves.

Technical limitations in the use and positioning of video equipment demand that the coach assess in advance which areas or aspects should be the focus. The recording technicians, who ought to be able to control the technical side of things, should understand the coach's wishes.

Praise as motivation can be conducted through a video recording. When prediscussed or trained situations succeed—perhaps culminating in a goal—it is edifying to show selected scenes. This will also familiarize the players with the rewards of training systematically and of trying out preplanned actions during matches.

# Types of Training and Session Organization

There is a saying that applies to all learning: "Theory is one thing; practice is quite another." Playing games, the players will learn some tactical aspects by themselves, but if the coach desires long-lasting improvement and developmental possibilities from a team point of view, it is necessary to work systematically. During the different phases of development, certain types of training are more effective than others in focusing the learning. The following deals with the various types of training and organization coaches can implement in training sessions. Several may complement each other.

## Type 1 : Illustration Work

### Method

The implementation of defined movement patterns and actions. See figure 4.1.

### Aim

For players to memorize reactions in terms of moves and skills in specific situations.

### Usage

Repeating an action many times is vital in establishing specific reaction patterns in a player. This type of exercise is used in both technical and tactical training, usually with little or no pressure. Correspondingly, this is an opportunity to take great care with details and timing between game actions, especially in tactical training. This type of training tends to work most effectively in developing teamwork between two or three players. Coaches can use illustrative training as repetition drilling or to lead to more complex practices.

### Coaching Points

When a practice has been tried a couple of times, there is a tendency for the tempo to decrease. Avoid this; it limits effectiveness.

### Description

Number 10 moves toward 7, who plays 10. Number 10 passes back to 7, then sprints diagonally (behind 11). Number 7 passes the ball wide to 11, who dribbles toward the goal line and crosses the ball to 10 or 7.

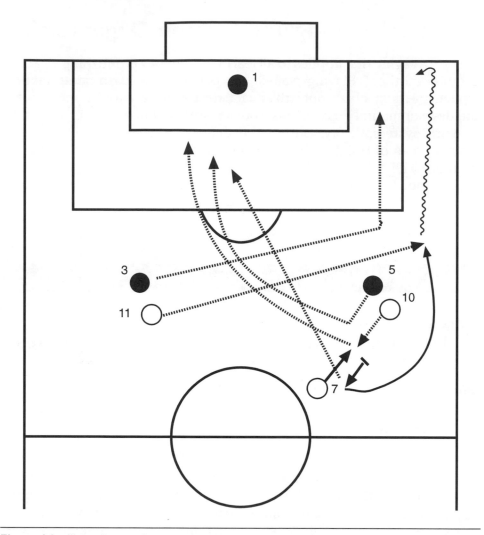

**Figure 4.1** Illustration work.

# Type 2: Conditional Play

### Method

Make specific conditions for the execution of the practice or game. See figure 4.2.

### Aim

Altering the rules of the game or the players' options accentuates certain movement patterns for the players, and many "replays" will take place.

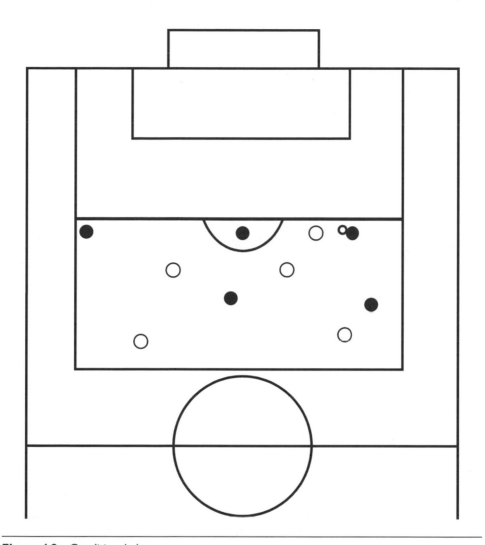

**Figure 4.2**   Conditional play.

## Usage

During the introductory and consolidating phases, particularly of specific tactical skills, the coach can intensify the players' observation of the training theme by implementing conditions in the practice or game. According to the aim of training, the conditions could be altering the dimensions of the field or playing the game with a limited number of touches on the ball. A good tool to use in this process is the "game wheel" (see figure 4.3).

New coaches often find it difficult to design a conditioning practice that works well. However, if they observe and become experienced in the ways new conditions create new practices, coaches will soon

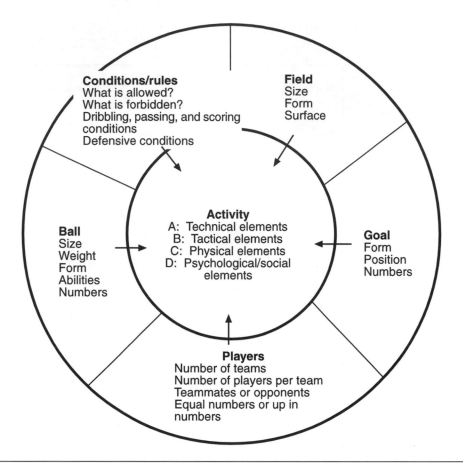

**Figure 4.3** The game wheel.

discover that they achieve better, goal-oriented training sessions than if they simply copy other coaches' practice sessions.

### Coaching Points

A new conditioning game needs time to take effect. The players must have time to adapt to the game before they can gain fully from the training. Try not to make too many minor adjustments during the game; this will easily confuse the players.

### Description

A team is only allowed to play the ball to the other zone if all the players from that team are positioned inside the zone from which the ball is arriving.

# Type 3: Pressure Training

**Method**

To work intensively for a short period of time with a limited tactical object. See figure 4.4.

**Aim**

To familiarize players with game conditions and available reaction time for tactical actions.

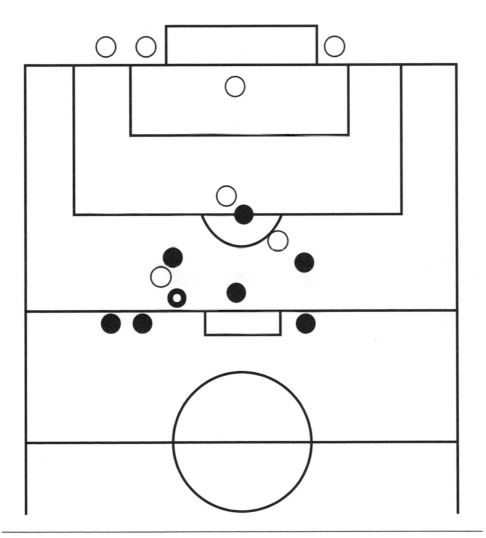

**Figure 4.4**  Pressure training.

## Usage

In decisive game situations, there is no time for long deliberations on how to resolve situations. By organizing practices and games that, isolated and with many repetitions, shorten players' reaction time in making tactical decisions, the coach will be able to practice selected tactical reaction patterns to prepare for match conditions. Pressure training is often used in shooting practices inside the penalty box. Practices involve players in pressure situations where they need to react quickly. An example might be a 45-second work ratio, where players pass in turn to a teammate in the center of a circle of players, and the central player's task is to meet the ball early to practice a wall backpass. Placing a cone further ahead for the central player to run past when passing the ball back applies even more pressure.

## Coaching Points

Playing under pressure can be physically demanding, so it is vital that this work not go on too long.

## Description

Three players from each team take turns playing one minute at a time. The players have a maximum of two touches on the ball, and after gaining possession of it, a team may exchange no more than five passes before shooting on goal.

# Type 4: Shadow Play

## Method

Effect buildup, consolidation play, and breakthrough with or without a limited number of opponents. See figure 4.5.

## Aim

To give players an understanding of general offensive running patterns or specific tactical skills (e.g., two-touch soccer).

## Usage

In 11-versus-11 situations, it becomes difficult to view the different phases of the team's tactical running as a whole. To gain an ideal picture of the system and the anticipated running patterns or tactical demands, players can play against imaginary opponents. By laying out 10 or more cones on the field at random, the coach can add small impediments to the passes.

**Figure 4.5**   Shadow play.

# Type 5: Focus Play—Specific Training

### Method

Focus on a specific tactical function with one or two players. See figure 4.6.

### Aim

To improve players' tactical action.

### Usage

When a player is unsure what to do tactically in a particular circumstance, the situation may need to be taken out and examined in specific training. The coach works with the player—along with necessary team members, some of whom will serve as opponents—within the actual playing arena on the pitch. This specific training must gradually evolve into the normal game situation or into a realistic phase of the match situation.

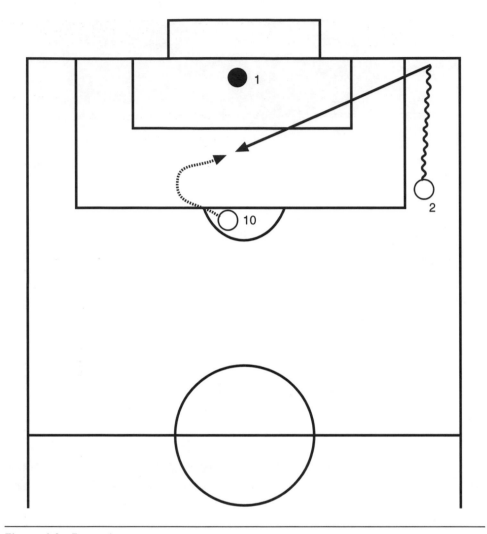

**Figure 4.6** Focus play.

## Keywords

Crossing player: Passing position • Awareness • Pass
Shooting player: Timing of move • Running patterns • Teamwork

# Type 6: Phase Play

**Method**

Playing on half or three-quarters of the pitch, utilizing one or two phases of the team's attacking and defensive play. See figure 4.7.

**Aim**

To analyze the quality of teamwork and the execution of the chosen phases within situations resembling a match.

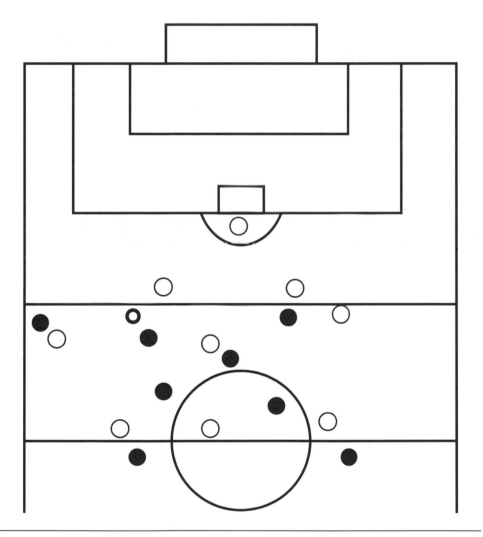

**Figure 4.7**  Phase play.

## Usage

Phase play is an important type of tactical training, and the most popular practice is defense versus attack on a one-half or three-quarter pitch with full-size goals. This is a way to practice group or team tactical elements, and assess and discuss them in relation to actual situations. In addition, in these situations, the coach can use some of the other methods of instruction, such as follow-up guidance and freeze instruction.

## Coaching Points

Normally, the attacking group is most motivated by the games. For this reason, it is important to set challenging goals for the defending team and to acknowledge their attainment; for example, points can be awarded for intercepted balls.

In this game, the players become accustomed to making sure they are aware of their teammates' positions and to maintaining communication between the units. The game also works on the transitional phases from defense to attack and vice versa as, following either losing or winning possession of the ball, all players are rapidly forced to participate appropriately in attacking or defensive play.

# Type 7: Grid Training

## Method

Training practices within a limited area.

## Aim

To practice some basic technical-tactical skills.

## Usage

The grid system uses a marked-off area with dimensions of about 10 m by 10 m. Grid training is beneficial, for example, for four-versus-two play with limitations on ball touches, and one-on-one challenging, because of the limited playing area. The players learn both to play themselves out of tight situations and to establish marking in closed areas. The tactical demands in a limited game situation become clear, and the coach has a good overall view of the work being done.

## Coaching Points

One possibility is to have permanent grid marking. This will help in organizing small-sided games, since the practices can be started and altered with ease by changing the size of the pitch.

# Types of Instruction

Following are descriptions of the three different types of instruction that aid the session.

## Type 8: Freeze Instruction

### Method

Stop the game immediately.

### Aim

To freeze a game situation to be discussed.

### Usage

It can be very helpful to freeze a game to point out and demonstrate a tactical situation. This method must be used to deal with a relevant training theme; utilize the break either to emphasize the correct method or point out problems in the handling of a specific situation. The break should allow a brief elaboration and an opportunity for the players involved to come forward with their opinions.

### Coaching Points

The players must know the signal for "freeze" and obey it.

# Type 9: Follow-Up Guidance—Coaching During Play

## Method

Advice and instruction from the coach to the players during practices and games.

## Aim

To support and guide a player's actions during play.

## Usage

When implementing new tactical systems or adjusting earlier styles of play, it can help for the coach to give regular input and guidance to the player regarding game situations. The coach's commentary means that the player receives direct feedback about the method of handling the task. The coach should not direct the player like a mechanical doll, but play the part of the analyzer. It can also be effective for the coach to play in a position alongside the player.

## Coaching Points

Some coaches are extremely active in their shouting and in the way they direct, and on the surface it will appear to the players that the coach is involved. However, if there is no real content in the one-way communication, it becomes a style that players will see through very quickly, which may lead to them losing some respect for the coach.

# Type 10: Managing Play on a Full-Size Pitch

## Method

Instructing during the game (11 versus 11) plus functioning as referee.

## Aim

To enhance the players' understanding of tactical conditions in relation to the entire game.

## Usage

Playing on a full-size pitch is vital in order to convert the work of training to a competitive context, the "match of the day." It is, in particular, natural to focus on the major tactical points in the approaching match and to give the anticipated starting lineup appropriate playing time. During the game, the coach will give various instructions and may make use of some of the different instructional methods, as described here. If this is the last 11-versus-11 game before a match, it is important not to interrupt the game too often.

## Coaching Points

The referee function should normally be enforced strictly as a reminder of the competitive milieu. The players, especially the second-team players, will easily lose motivation if they only hear the whistle every now and then. The players should normally be able to referee themselves, but just as part of the preparation for an approaching match, the function of the referee should be underlined.

# CHAPTER 5

# Coaching

Coaching is the general term used to describe the way a coach performs the role of working to improve the team's performance. A coach's methods can be deemed successful when the team and the individual players utilize their resources to the utmost, and the individual player, as well as the team, has acquired new options for action.

Coaching is based to a lesser extent on the normal concept of training and its planning, but the idea is to utilize the player's options to meet specific demands. This concerns the different ways in which the outside soccer world perceives the aims of, and the different interests, problems, conflicts and expectations in relation to, soccer performance.

Coaching is about the interaction between the coach and the player as a human being. This chapter limits itself to describing only those functions related to the area of tactics. Coaching can be described in relation to the activities before, during, and after a match.

The coach's aim should be to stabilize the mental state of the players to gain their optimum performance. This stabilization occurs primarily on a psychological level so that concentration can be maintained and re-established even under strained conditions and situations in a match.

## Coaching Roles

There are several ways to act as a coach. Matches on television quickly demonstrate different types of coaches. It is now not simply the "official" appearance that paints a reliable picture of the coach, even if that is a picture often in the spectator's view. The daily coaching routine can easily be somewhat different from the official picture. It is therefore essential to outline the way coaching management generally will take place. Scandinavian research focusing on 25 successful elite soccer coaches and 25 unsuccessful ones describes those criteria that characterize a successful coach. This is someone who is skilled in planning, who sets up goals and sticks to them. The successful coach prioritizes what to focus on—and what should be avoided. This coach is effective in disseminating information, is always well-informed, has the ability to remain composed, and can empathize at all times with the players on the team. It is also essential to add that the good coach does not just know about soccer but also has a knowledge of society. This person is curious and understands how to collect information. Finally, the coach has a serious interest in people and is therefore group-oriented, with an aim more toward teamwork than to competition within the team. It is rare to find people who possess all of the above qualities and who also have suitable practical experience. Today, most clubs establish coaching teams, where each coach involved contributes a few of the above-mentioned skills.

# Methods of Training

The coach normally has a set method of conducting training; however, it is always sensible to assess constantly what one is doing and be prepared to adjust it. All preparation and development of training should be decided by four factors: the coach, the players, the demands of the individual game, and the situation. These four elements influence each other and, thereby, the development of a set training component. Here, they are incorporated into a diagram that demonstrates the use of different methods of instruction (see figure 5.1).

The diagram shows the basics of analyzing, and even preparing, one's own methods of instruction. It can also function as a support tool for less experienced coaches.

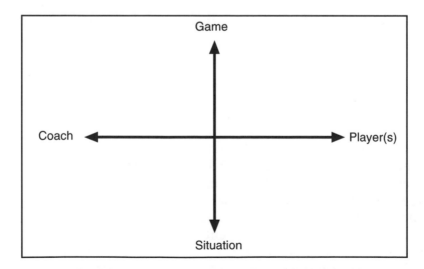

**Figure 5.1**    The four factors that determine method of instruction.

The following model shows how different methods and types of instruction can be varied, depending on where the priorities lie between the four factors.

## Training Aspect One: Train the Practice

When training should focus on the game's basic tactical needs, the coach becomes the expert (see figure 5.2). The issue here is the set of preconditions important in order for the players to be proficient in the game's tactical demands at a certain level—for example, organization of marking and improvement of wall-passes.

The choice of practices should give both the players and the coach the opportunity to focus on the detail. The organization of the practice requires that it is precise and unequivocal.

Based on the coach's expertise, it is the practice and the details of the practice that are important, and the coach will therefore profit by making use of the usual direct training method and formal training principles.

The method of instruction consists of four phases:

1. the practice is demonstrated as a whole;
2. the practice is clarified, focusing on the decisive elements needed for mastery;
3. the practice is demonstrated again; and
4. the players practice while the coach gives them feedback on their efforts.

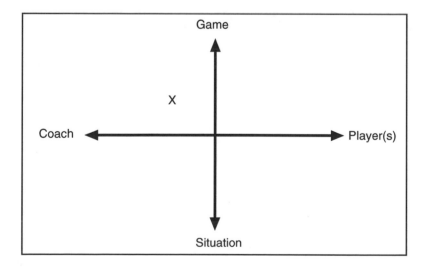

**Figure 5.2**  Train the practice.

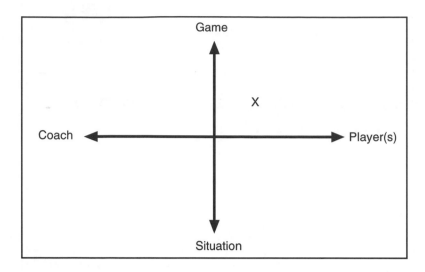

**Figure 5.3** Train the players' options.

## Training Aspect Two: Train the Players' Options

When the purpose of training is to develop the players' soccer skills, the object is to stimulate their developmental processes. As a basis, the coach should choose and develop practices or activities that are suitably challenging for the players. (See figure 5.3.)

Training can start off along fairly loosely defined lines, which are continually adjusted according to the players' reactions. The coach should assess things from a long-term perspective.

The coach's role is that of starter and guide. The important aspect of leading the training is to give a lot of feedback to the players regarding their problem solving. It is equally important for the players to follow the coach's assessment. The best way is to use the functional training principle, which builds on the understanding that training of skills and teamwork should occur in a situation as close to a match as possible.

## Training Aspect Three: Interpreting Situations

A team will experience times when psychological factors have such an impact on the climate of the session that the coach must adapt the choice of content and style to the situation (see figure 5.4). Teammates can be set against each other—"young against old," for example—to increase competitiveness among the players. Another example is model training, where the coach tries in the session to emulate the external factors that seem to be influencing performance. Long periods of defeat or victory can contribute to the strain of the training environment and can be difficult for the coach to handle. Even though many will be of the opinion that constant victories are a good problem, they will still affect the training performance.

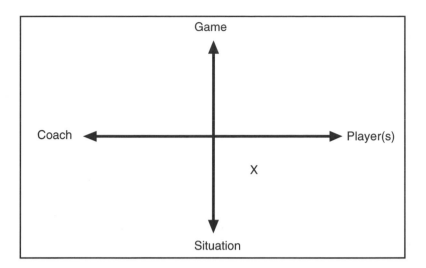

**Figure 5.4** Interpreting situations.

More often than not, the effect is positive, but if the coach is not careful to create balance in the players' self-confidence, the positive effects may rapidly disappear. When the coach is completely tied up with the coaching job, it can be difficult at times to get any distance from the hullabaloo. It is important for a coach to be able to sense the psychological climate of the team and be able to adjust the "dosage" and style of training in accordance with any tension.

Since different situations can result in stress in the training and playing atmosphere, there is no "best" method of instruction. It is the coach's identification ability that is decisive in the outcome of such situations. By coming up with surprises in practice or in match preparation, the coach can perhaps break the monotony.

## Training Aspect Four: Maintenance Training

The coach defines certain training and match routines. These could include, for example, a set warm-up program and a game that do not require any explanation since they have been performed many times before. In these situations, the coach becomes a safety facilitator. It is important that, between other practices, the players do have periods where they can go through well-known routines in order to strengthen something at which they excel. See figure 5.5.

# Working as a Coach

The numerous functions that make up the coach's role can be summarized in a schematic index (see table 5.1).

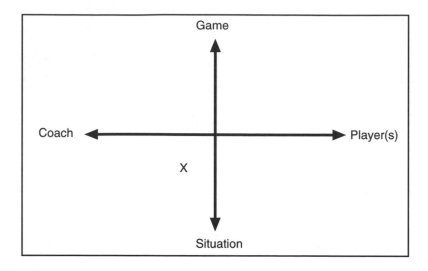

**Figure 5.5**   Maintenance training.

## Table 5.1  The Coach's Role

**Before a match**

**1. Feedback on the previous match (the day after)**

Response to media reports – ad hoc situations (from a long-term point of view, e.g., tactical development – positive feedback, possibly through the use of a video)

Injured players (contact – action: mental level – risk – the tough and lonely struggle – rapidly feeling an outsider – dropped from the team – opportunity for involvement in the training)

Recovery training (not just physically)

**2. Preparation for the next match**

Prioritizing (see table 3.1 on page 52 in chapter 3 for analyzing opponents, possibly using a video)

Training content (specific conditions: dead-ball situations – personal attitude and assessment in relation to the previous and coming match)

Psychological adaptation (tension)

2. **Preparation for the next match** *(continued)*

   Determining the aim of the team – what we will achieve, including building up the confidence of individual players – motivation (for example, against weak opponents)

3. **Team selection**

   Procedure (contact especially with unselected players)

4. **Final training**

   Aim

   Lifestyle (understanding of nutrition, etc.)

5. **Team meeting, tactics meeting, tactical presentation**

   Time, stretching, form of presentation—for example, visual aids

## On match day

1. **Before the match**

   Meeting procedure/transport – perhaps a tactical presentation or repetition

   Warm-up (normal procedure), personal contact, especially regarding the strong points of the team

   Pep talk (concentration)

2. **During the match**

   Communication (tactical adjustments – sign language – methods of communication)

   Disruption (referee error – injuries – substitution)

   Intervention (tactical), for example, the assessment of the tactical performance

3. **Halftime**

   Tactical directions and individual guidance

4. **Second half**

   Specific situations (intervention)

   Communication (awareness of time)

   Select penalty shooters (cup matches)

   Perspective (evaluation)

5. **After the match**

   First reaction, including that of the media

   Player situation (especially injuries)

   Player assessment—swift feedback (especially for debuting players, new players, players who failed)

# Team Hierarchy

As a soccer player, one becomes increasingly aware of oneself as a player, and of one's importance and role on the team.

This manifests itself particularly on senior teams. It is normal, therefore, for a hierarchy to emerge in a team composed of younger players, talented players, and more experienced ones. A player's position within this hierarchy goes primarily by age, performance, and personal attitude (authority) on and off the pitch. A hierarchy can enhance a team's performance, but it can also hinder a team's chances. This progression depends on how the hierarchical roles have been developed and the way they are managed. The advantage of a hierarchy is that it has a clear distribution of roles. Individual players know what is expected of their actions and performance, and what they can expect from their teammates. The hierarchy demonstrates its benefits predominantly in pressure situations. The players highest in the hierarchy must act with drive and use their weight of experience as a lead for the less experienced. Both during practice and in the match, a well-functioning hierarchy will be an invaluable support tool for a coach. A team's psychological state shows in the way the players interact with each other during and after training or a match. It is important to value the leading players as advisors while simultaneously putting a certain amount of responsibility on their shoulders.

The hierarchy should not simply take the form of the younger players fetching water, carrying the soccer balls, carrying the goalposts, and looking out for the bags. This is the good-natured sort of ranking found in most clubs. The youngest players' practical tasks can help them a great deal in adapting to a sense of their responsibility within the team, especially as some newly promoted players have difficulty accustoming themselves to a position different from that they were used to, having been "stars" in their glorious youth careers. Internal influence from other players carries more weight than if the coach undertakes the "upbringing" process alone.

The hierarchical process can be hampered by some common situations. The experience of bureaucracies demonstrates that hierarchies have a tendency to stagnate. The highest level fights displacement. If highly ranked players maintain their privileges without playing with the same competence, dissatisfaction will rapidly develop, and conflicts may arise. For a soccer team, the aim should be to work toward a flat hierarchy, which lies in the philosophy of team building.

Development of cliques will oppose movement toward a flat hierarchy, because the clique will always have first say in decisions, regardless of whether the decisions concern the whole team. Teams will thus break into two or more groups.

# Team Building

When people in an organization want to work together on set tasks, organizational psychologists use the term "team building" to describe a vital part of the establishment of a properly functioning group.

Team building, in the context of soccer, refers to the relationship between the coach and players, as well as among the players themselves. All should feel that they are given the opportunity to utilize their particular talents and experiences, that they receive support from each other, and that there is a good atmosphere within the team. Team building is about the way a group is developed so that the individual feels that "it is not MY team—it is OUR team."

The process of helping the players to reach this awareness and position may be encouraged by various means. The vital basis for developing common strength lies in communication and information. A properly functioning group exhibits interaction. Members have the opportunity and the will to express themselves. Mutual acknowledgment of each other's actions is important; they must be considered meaningful and relevant in order for the team to succeed. Within this, there should also be an understanding and acknowledgment of feelings and self-esteem. The work of the team is a primary topic of communication. The way in which the group's resources are best utilized in terms of this—the preplanned goals—should be clarified. The goals should be clear and obvious so that the players can participate in working toward their attainment. Equally, it should be clear what the group expects of the individual, and vice versa.

There are several ways of promoting this team development. When making the final selection of tactics, the coach can bring into a team meeting the players' assessments of how everyone can best contribute to the optimum fulfillment of the tactic. As an example, successful pressure play can be achieved when individual players are clear about both their own roles and their context within patterns of action of the other players. In discussing qualities of style of play, one automatically learns the players' self-assessments and thoughts about the efforts of other players.

# Competitive Training in Team Building

The psychological burden on players during a match is difficult to reproduce under normal training conditions. It is particularly useful to prepare for those times when the team has fallen behind. One way of focusing on the psychological burden during training is to use games with a strong competitive element. Here we have described two such games. Each game consists of four periods of play for, say, 10 minutes at a time, played for prizes—for example, soda pops. The competitive factor during the third and especially the fourth period of play puts pressure on the players. If the game ends as a draw, the match is decided by a penalty shoot-out.

# Game 1

### Pitch

One-half pitch with two full-size goals.

### Players

Sixteen—eight versus eight, including a goalkeeper for each team.

### Description

Normal play. After four minutes of play in the fourth period, the side that was in the lead at the end of the third period has a goal taken away every two minutes until the team scores.

### Coaching Points

The method of scoring in the fourth period is part of maintaining the intensity in the match. The rule means that the result cannot be "carried" home even if a team has the lead, and that even if a team is behind, it is still motivated to prevent further scoring.

# Game 2

### Pitch

One-quarter pitch with one small goal (handball goal/minigoal) and one full-size goal.

### Players

Four versus four, plus a goalkeeper who is restricted to the full-size goal.

### Description

Normal play in four periods of six minutes each. There are no goalkeeper privileges at the small goal; no one may act as a goalkeeper. The same scoring rules apply as in the first game, but the goalkeeper at the full-size goal remains in position when switching halves.

**Conditions**

Man-marking.

**Coaching Points**

The game focuses on attention to marking and on an overall view.

# CHAPTER 6

# Dead-Ball Situations

A dead-ball situation can be defined as any time in a match when the ball is put into play after a stop in the action. During a soccer match, various situations arise when play is restarted. On an international level, a team has, on average, something like four kickoffs, nine goal kicks, 20 throw-ins, 15 free kicks, and 10 corner kicks, plus one penalty kick every three matches. In the attacking zone, there is an average total of 20 dead-ball situations for a team, per match.

Research from the final rounds of the 1990 and 1994 World Cups as well as the 1996 European Championships in England show that goals as a result of dead-ball situations, free kicks and corner kicks in particular, make up a large percentage of the total scoring (see table 6.1).

## Table 6.1   Goals Resulting From Dead-Ball Situations

| Event | Goals | Goals following a dead-ball situation | Goals following a free kick* | Goals following a corner kick |
|---|---|---|---|---|
| 1990 World Cup | 115 | 32% | 12% | — |
| 1994 World Cup | 141 | 25% | 8% | — |
| 1996 European Championships | 64 | 27% | 6% | 17% |

*The figures for free kicks include goals scored from combination play.

Greece's goal from a free kick, during a World Cup qualifier against Denmark, shows the importance of good organization in situations where the opposition has a free kick outside the penalty area.

# Offense

If it is already known that certain situations arise regularly during a match, it makes sense to improve the possibility of benefiting from them. This can be done by practicing dead-ball combinations, in which the players carry out rehearsed moves.

Aims of practicing dead-ball situations include the following:

- To increase the chances of a dead-ball situation leading to a finishing opportunity, or for the team to keep the ball under control
- To create confidence in players who are involved in dead-ball situations

The planning and training of dead-ball combinations can be divided into four phases:

- Choice of combination
- Specific training
- Training in games
- Use of games on a full-size pitch

## Choice of Combination

In the first phase, the team must decide what dead-ball combinations to use. These decisions can quite easily be made in conjunction with the players. Dead-ball situations lend themselves to the involvement of players and utilization of their experiences, because the situation is clear. The choice, of course, depends on which players are available. It will do no good, for example, to plan a throw-in combination where the ball can be headed on from the six-yard box if there are no players who can throw the ball that far. It is also usually a good idea to choose combinations that require limited or no arrangements to be made between players during the game. This will mean that the team only needs to concentrate on carrying out the action practiced in training and agreed upon prior to the match. Nor are opponents given any information about the combination for which the team is preparing. For example, although often seen, it is inappropriate for the player taking the corner kick to raise his arm if the cross is going to the far side of the penalty area. The first time opponents see the sign, they will be extra observant, and next time they will read the simple code and be ready with countermeasures.

## Specific Training

After the choice phase, the coach should decide which players to use in individual dead-ball combinations. Those players are then selected for specific training, in which the individual moves are analyzed in detail. A keyword in dead-ball combinations is timing, with players' movements properly adjusted timewise. It is partly for this reason that the players must concentrate fully during training; therefore, it is appropriate to start off with only a few players initially, adding more gradually once the original players have learned their moves. In order to make sure that the players fully understand the object of their runs, it may also be necessary to introduce some defenders at a later stage. This should be limited as much as possible, because they will often get bored and benefit only minimally from the training. In some cases, they can actually distract those players who are actively involved in rehearsing the combination. When practicing dead-ball situations, the most important training aspect is the individual timing between the players, not the kicks or throw-ins that start the plays. They can be practiced individually.

This phase of practicing dead-ball situations is often not particularly demanding from a physical point of view, and it may be put before or after normal training time, or on days when training intensity should be low, such as the day before a match. If this aspect is carried out as a part of normal training, the coach must ensure that another training activity is under way for those players who are not involved in the dead-ball situation.

## Training in Games

During the specific training of a dead-ball combination, the players only have their own runs and the decision of when to act to consider. But can they remember all these things in the heat of the moment? Will every player be able to concentrate on the task? To facilitate the transition from specific training to usage in a match, it is useful to incorporate dead-ball combinations (one at a time) into a game. In this phase, the players must quickly learn how to adapt from game conditions to concentrating on their runs in the relevant dead-ball situation. The player putting the ball back into play must, in addition, get an idea of when it is appropriate to use one combination instead of another (depending on the positions of the opponents, weather conditions, etc.). This phase also gives players an idea of how dead-ball situations work when opponents become involved, which, in turn, gives rise to opportunities for fine-tuning. Furthermore, this "testing out" in a game can be used to orient the rest of the players on the team, so that they understand what has been practiced and see that they are not positioning themselves inappropriately in a combination.

The training of a dead-ball situation in a game can be any time during the session, but it is appropriate to give this phase some time immediately following the introduction of a new dead-ball combination.

Be aware that no matter how a game is constructed in the training of dead-ball situations, some abnormal situations will occur, because the game will be disrupted more than usual. Therefore, the game should not be longer than 20 minutes, and it is important for the players to be informed of the aim of the game. At times, games have been used where the coach whistles regularly for free kicks or, with free kicks, moves the ball from one end of the pitch to the other, to practice free-kick combinations. This type of game may be used, but it is not recommended, since the opposing team often loses interest in the match, which causes the dead-ball situations to become unrealistic.

In the descriptions of individual dead-ball situations, we present a game that may be used to practice the relevant dead-ball combination. Here we have provided an example of a game that can be used for practicing combinations for all types of dead-ball situations.

# Practice Game for Dead-Ball Combinations

**Pitch**

About two-fifths pitch with a halfway line and two full-size goals.

**Players**

Fourteen—seven versus seven, including a goalkeeper on each team.

**Organization**

The players involved in the relevant dead-ball situation all play on the same team (the "dead-ball team"). The dead-ball team attacks toward the penalty area (see figure 6.1).

**Description**

Normal play. If the dead-ball team wins the ball in the opposition's half, the team is awarded the ball in the situation to be trained.

**Scoring**

As normal.

**Variations**

1. The dead-ball team finishes its attack after gaining the ball on the opposition's half of the field, from where the dead ball is given.
2. Each time the ball goes out of play on the opposition's half of the field—for example, through a throw-in or free kick—it is put back into play using the dead-ball situation being practiced.

**Coaching Points**

It is an advantage, but not strictly necessary, for the opposing team to be unaware of the relevant dead-ball situation. At the end of a game, the dead-ball situation can be used to explain to the other players in

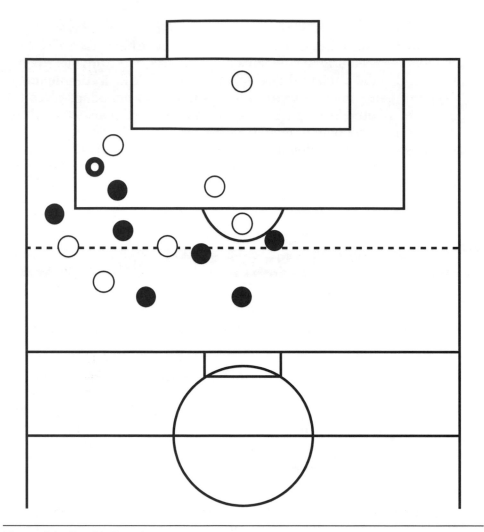

**Figure 6.1** Dead-ball combination practice.

detail which combinations were practiced. The coach should then allow time to hear suggestions for improvement from the rest of the players. With the size of the pitch, the number of dead-ball situations that arise can be controlled to a certain extent. The coach should, however, be careful not to make the pitch too small, as many un-realistic situations can arise from this, wasting a lot of time.

## Keywords

Concentration • Consistency • Timing

The corner kick formation for the Danish national team with two strong players in the air at the front post.

## Individual Dead-Ball Situations

The following pages cover each dead-ball situation and suggest examples of combinations. It is important to remember, however, only to use dead-ball situations that are suitable for an individual team.

## Kickoffs

The kickoff can be used tactically and psychologically. Starting the match by kicking the ball forward to the opposition's line of defense and immediately putting pressure on the defenders can signal: "We want something today." Should this pressure lead to a defender's losing the ball, it may result in the opposition having a bad start to the match. The kickoff is likewise exploitable at the start of the second half or when the opposition has scored, where the pressure on the opposition can remove some of the despondency and hopelessness so often visible in such situations. For a kickoff to succeed, it is vital that the attackers are going 100 percent for the ball and that the rest of the team push up aggressively.

It can be valuable to have a rehearsed combination to play the ball forward from kickoff and maintain it in the opposition's defensive zone. One difficulty in relation to the kickoff is that the forwards are positioned around the halfway line, and all the opponent's players are in their own half. It is therefore necessary to quickly push the attackers forward past the opponent's attacking and midfield players. The following is an example of how this can be done.

## Combination at Kickoff

**Organization**

> Two players stand by the ball (numbers 7 and 8). Three players stand at the halfway line (numbers 9, 10, and 11). A player is positioned some meters outside the center circle (number 6). See figure 6.2.

**Description**

> Number 8 passes to 7, who plays the ball back to 6. Meanwhile, numbers 9, 10, and 11 have run at maximum speed toward the opposition's penalty area. Numbers 7 and 8 are also running forward at a high speed. The rest of the players follow at least as far as the halfway line. With a one-touch pass, number 6 tries to reach 11 just outside the penalty box. Number 11 tries to head the ball, either into the penalty box to 9 or 10, across to 8, or back to 7.

**Coaching Points**

> Number 6 must try to pass to 11 so that the ball lands right in front of the opposition's right fullback/marking player. Numbers 9 and 10

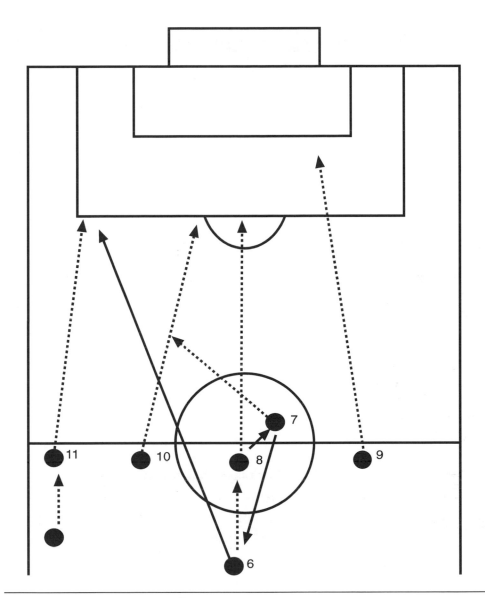

**Figure 6.2**  Combination at kickoff.

must move directly toward and into the penalty area. If 11 becomes embroiled in a struggle with the defenders for the ball, the attacker and midfielders must help to close down the area. It is important for the whole team to push up, thereby putting pressure on the opposition.

## Keywords

Point of arrival • Push forward • Squeezing/closing down

# Practice Game for the Kickoff Combination

**Pitch**

About three-fifths pitch incorporating the halfway line on a normal pitch, and two full-size goals.

**Players**

Sixteen—eight versus eight, including a goalkeeper for each team.

**Organization**

The players involved in the kickoff play are all on the same team (the "dead-ball team"). The dead-ball team attacks in the direction of the penalty area. See figure 6.3.

**Description**

Normal play. When the dead-ball team has a goal kick or the opposition scores, all players must be positioned behind the halfway line, while all opposition players must be in their own half. The dead-ball team starts with the ball at the center spot.

**Scoring**

Score as normal.

**Variations**

1. Once the kickoff has been taken, the goalkeeper is not permitted to intervene until another player has touched the ball.
2. Teams are allowed a maximum of five passes before finishing.
3. Same as variation 2, except every player has a maximum of three touches each time in contact with the ball.

**Coaching Points**

Timing between the players involved should be emphasized. If using a long forward pass to the penalty, focus attention on the quality of the kick and the run from the receiving player.

Variation 1 can be utilized if the goalkeeper, knowing where the dead-ball team is going to put the ball, moves forward to intercept it. Utilize variations 2 and 3 to increase the number of kickoffs and the aggressiveness of the players.

## Keywords

Point of arrival • Advancement • Closing down

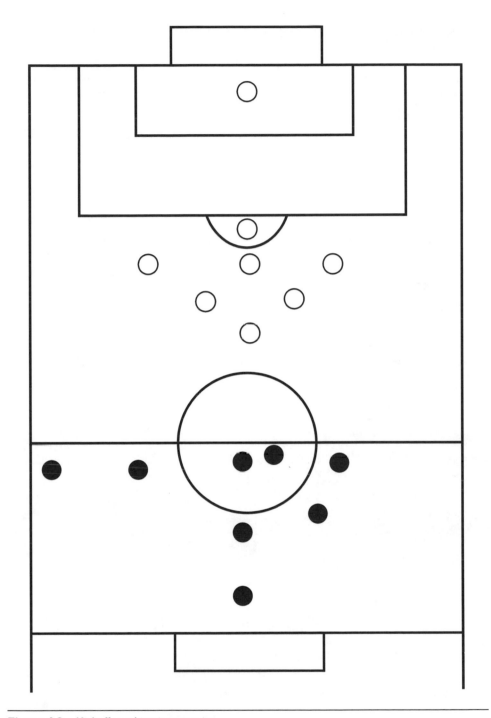

**Figure 6.3** Kickoff combination practice.

## Throw-Ins

A throw-in is a delivery to a team member and must, therefore, have the same qualities as a pass using the foot. However, a throw-in is often more difficult to work, which is not simply due to the fact that the ball must be thrown over the head. In most cases, part of the reason is that the players are not sufficiently aware of the importance of accuracy in the throw-in. It is vital for the ball to be thrown with a force and angle that gives the player on the receiving end the best chance of controlling the pass or playing the ball into open space. It is also extremely important that the team members spread out, so as to hinder the opposition's marking and to create free spaces, which can be exploited once the ball is received following the throw-in. In addition, the player receiving the ball should maintain an appropriate distance from the player who is taking the throw-in. A commonly observed error is when a player sets up in a position too close to the player taking the throw-in, thereby increasing the play's difficulty, partly in the throw, and partly in controlling the ball afterward.

A long throw-in or corner kick to the far post can be an effective weapon of attack; it is used occasionally by the Danish national team, with Kim Vilfort as the main proponent.

Taking a throw-in quickly is often an advantage. This exploits the fact that the opposition's marking in the area is not yet complete. It is usually a good idea to throw to a teammate who can immediately bring the ball forward.

The thrower should immediately reenter the game. In situations where players are closely marked, the unmarked position of the player taking the throw-in can be exploited; an example would be by throwing the ball to a marked player, who makes a one-touch pass back to the thrower. For this to succeed, the player receiving the ball must be a certain distance from the thrower, and the receiving player's run and the throw-in must be well-timed.

If the team has one or more players capable of making long throws, they can exploit it in the attacking zone. The long throw-in can also create space for the other team members on the short throw-in.

Usually, it is a good idea to concentrate lots of players in the penalty area to create pressure and disturbance in front of the opposition's goal. A player can set up in front of the goal area with the primary task of heading or flicking the ball on from the throw-in. Because of the unpredictable direction the ball may go, the defenders' task is difficult. The other members of the team take positions partly inside and partly outside the six-yard box. They should accelerate toward the ball when the flick-on player makes contact. It is important that the player heads toward the far post, where a correctly executed flick-on will create big problems for the defenders in the area (see also flick-on at a corner kick). Another good idea is to position a player close to the goalkeeper to restrict the defender's vision and freedom of movement. That player must be careful to avoid fouls or running into an offside position.

Following are two examples of long throw-in combinations.

## Long Throw-Ins I

### Organization

See figure 6.4. A player (number 7) makes a throw-in. A player (number 9) is at the front post, while another player (11) stands two to three paces behind 9. A player (10) takes position in front of the goalkeeper, while two players (numbers 5 and 8) stand just outside the six-yard box. A player (6) takes up a position around the penalty spot. A player (2) gets into position right in the corner of the penalty area. The remaining players are positioned inside or just outside the penalty area.

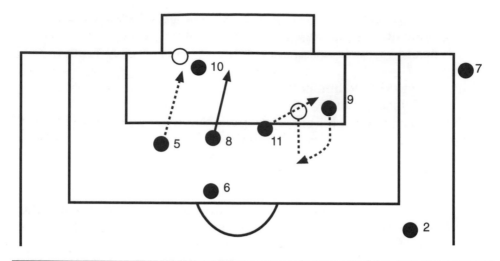

**Figure 6.4**   Long throw-ins example 1.

## Description

Number 9 moves away from the front post just before 7 finishes the run-up and tries to bring along the marking player (if the marking player doesn't come along, 9 will be free), creating space for 11, who can flick the ball on to 5, 6, 8, or 10 standing in the middle. Numbers 5, 6, and 8 must move toward the six-yard box the instant 11 makes contact with the ball.

## Variations

1. Number 9 runs toward the player taking the throw-in, to create the option for a short throw-in.
2. A short throw-in comes to 9, who passes to 7 or possibly 2.
3. Number 7 fakes a long throw-in to tempt the goalkeeper forward, then throws short to 2, who has moved out toward 7 and on receiving the ball passes immediately back to 7, or inside.

## Coaching Points

It is important that 9 moves just before 7 releases the ball, so that 11 can utilize the free space 9 creates. If 9 starts too late, there will be no room for 11; if 9 starts too early, the space will be closed off. Often, the first phase of a throw-in (to 11) succeeds and the second phase (the moves of the other players) fails. It is therefore necessary to emphasize that 5, 6, and 8 must concentrate on stepping in during the second phase. This is greatly important to the success of the throw-in combination.

During variations 1 and 2, number 9 must run quickly toward 7, who must assess whether to throw the ball to 11 or short to 9, depending partly on how free 9 is of the marker.

In variation 3, number 2 should imply a disinterest in receiving the ball and, say, run slightly toward the penalty area, then make a run toward number 7 as 7 approaches the sideline. It is important for the accuracy of number 7's throw that number 2 accelerate early enough.

# Long Throw-Ins 2

### Organization

See figure 6.5. A player (number 2) takes the throw-in. Three tall players are side by side at the near post. A player (9) stands in front of the goalkeeper, while three players (6, 7, and 8) are just outside the six-yard box. The others take positions in or around the penalty area.

### Description

Number 2 throws to 5, 10, or 11. Numbers 6, 7, and 8 (far post) break toward the goal area the instant one of the other three touches the ball.

### Variations

1. More players at the near post.
2. A player running from the back breaks into the space ahead of the group of players.

### Coaching Points

The aim of the grouped players at the near post is to make the opposition's intervention more difficult and increase the probability

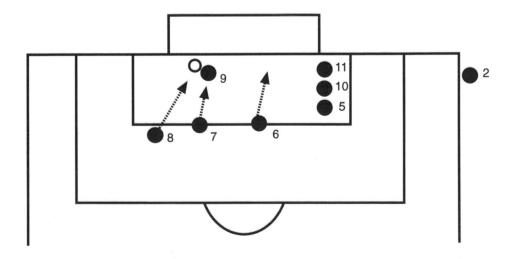

**Figure 6.5**   Long throw-ins example 2.

of a teammate receiving the throw. These players should be close enough together that the opposition cannot break through the wall and head the ball away.

In variation 2, the player running from defense should start the break immediately before the player taking the throw-in finishes the run-up.

# Practice Game for Long Throw-Ins

### Pitch

About one-third pitch with two full-size goals.

### Players

Fourteen—seven versus seven, including a goalkeeper on each team.

### Organization

The players involved in the throw-in combination are on the same team (the "dead-ball team"). The dead-ball team attacks toward the penalty area. See figure 6.6.

### Description

Normal play. If the dead-ball players get a throw-in or corner kick, they should carry out a throw-in from a position close to the opposition's goal line.

### Scoring

Goals can only be scored from a one-touch finish of either a header or a volley. A goal may be acknowledged, however, if it follows on from the use of the throw-in combination.

### Variations

1. A halfway line is introduced. If the dead-ball team wins the ball in the opposition's half, it is awarded a throw-in near the opposition's goal line.
2. A goal also gives the team a throw-in by the goal line.

### Coaching Points

If more than six players are involved in the throw-in combination, the most important players may be picked out for the first repetition. The pitch can subsequently be widened and the remaining players introduced. The players on the dead-ball team should, at every throw-in, concentrate solely on their own roles in the throw-in combination

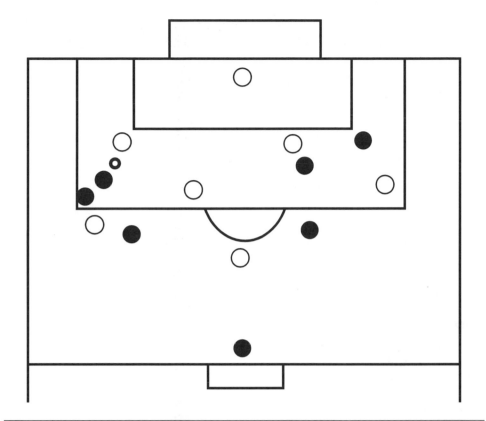

**Figure 6.6**   Long throw-in practice.

and ignore the risk the team runs by bringing many players forward. The scoring conditions are made partly because of the relatively large number of players gathered in a small area and partly because of the increased probability of the ball being played off the pitch.

Variations 1 and 2 can be used to increase the number of throw-ins, but to keep the game from getting too tedious for the opposition, the throw-ins should not occur too often.

## Corner Kicks

It is especially important during corner kicks to exploit the players' qualities. Is there a player who can pass a ball at head-height to the front post? Do we have players who are good in the air? But no matter what players are available, it is vital for a team to have different corner-kick combinations at its disposal, to maintain the elements of surprise and uncertainty for the opposition.

The examples of long throw-in combinations (pages 99-102) can— varied with long passes to players who are good in the air—also be utilized on corner kicks. Two additional examples follow.

# Corner Kicks I

## Organization

See figure 6.7. A player (number 6) takes the corner kick. A player (10) stands just in front of the near post. A player (7) is positioned near number 6. A player (9) is in front of the goalkeeper. A player (5) stands right outside the six-yard box in line with the front post. Two players (8 and 11) are in the penalty area. The rest of the players take up positions outside the penalty area.

## Description

Number 6 delivers to 10, who has made a break toward 6. Meanwhile, number 7 runs toward 6, then, at a certain moment, turns and runs into the penalty area. Number 10 passes the ball to 7, who attempts a finish or possibly passes to 8 or 11.

## Variations

1. Number 10 drops off. Number 6 plays 7, who dribbles along the goal line or passes with a backheel to 6, who has moved back down the pitch.

2. Number 6 passes the ball to 10, who turns and dribbles along the goal line or passes back to 6, who has dropped off.

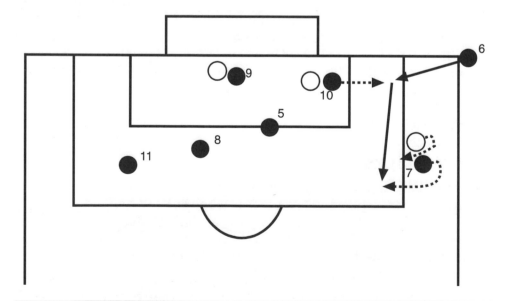

**Figure 6.7**   Corner kicks example 1.

3. Number 6 passes to 5, who has made a run into the free space created by 10. Number 5 flicks the ball on to 8, 9, or 11.

4. A long ball to 8 or 11.

## Coaching Points

The timing between 6, 7, and 10 is vital. Number 10's run toward 6 must wait until 6 is onto the ball. Number 7 must attract attention by, say, shouting to 6, so the direct opponent thinks 6 is about to pass to 7. Number 7 must start the run early to be able to turn the instant 6 crosses the ball. Number 7 must start off from farther away than 9—15 meters from the corner—to be marked, thus avoiding having an opponent enter the area to be utilized. It is important that 7 run slowly toward 6, thus taking the defender along, and that 7 does not get so close to 6 that the marking player can no longer follow. After turning, 7 should sprint, so as to lose the marker. The rest of the players must pay attention, so as not to block 7's area.

Variations 1 and 2 can be applied when 7 and 10 are not closely marked. During variation 2, 7 must take the marker along, so that 10 and 6 are allowed more playing space. In variation 3, 5 must start an angled run past the near post while 6 is taking the run-up to the ball. After variation 3 or 4 is complete, 7 and 10 must move into the penalty area to look for a finishing opportunity.

# Corner Kicks 2

## Organization

See figure 6.8. A player (number 6) takes the corner kick, and a player (7) stands right outside the "D" at the corner. Four players (numbers 8 through 11) are positioned in a diagonal line at the far post, while a player (5) takes up a position right in front of the goalkeeper. The remaining players stand on the edge of or just outside the penalty area.

## Description

Short corner. Number 6 passes to 7, who stops the ball, after which 6 runs forward and passes toward the far post to 8, 9, 10, or 11.

## Variations

1. After 7 has controlled the ball, 6 passes to a player outside the penalty area, after which that player should finish or pass to 8, 9, 10, or 11.

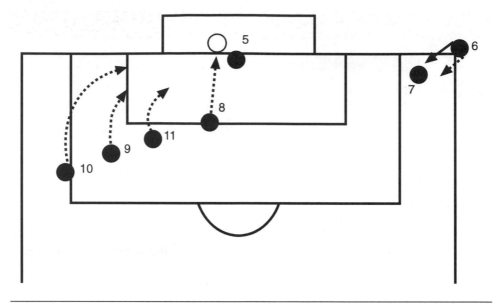

**Figure 6.8**   Corner kicks example 2.

2. Number 6 plays 7, who dribbles back, after which 7 plays 6 with a backheel.

3. Numbers 6 and 7 try to penetrate from the side.

**Coaching Points**

By first passing the ball to 7, number 6 has a better angle for reaching numbers 8, 9, 10, and 11. Furthermore, the goalkeeper will more often be conscious of the possibility of 6 finishing directly on goal, by which the opportunity for the goalkeeper to intercept the ball at the back of the six-yard box decreases. It is advisable to place the tallest player on the team second-to-last in the lineup (number 9), as the opposition will most likely position its best player in the air close to 9. Number 10 must start a curved run as number 6 takes the run-up, and then move behind 9 to receive the ball if it goes over the rest of the players.

Variation 1 can be utilized if the defenders focus their attention on the players in the penalty area or if the original format has been unsuccessful. Variations 2 and 3 are especially useful if the opposing team is only using one player to put pressure on both 6 and 7.

During variation 2, number 6 must quickly drop off behind 7, thus avoiding getting into an offside position. Following this, 6 must "hesitate" for an instant, and then make a run in the opposite direction when the ball is played. Numbers 6 and 7 must maintain appropriate distance: not too short—that would allow the defender to interfere when 6 receives the ball—but not too long, as this increases the risk of the defender gaining possession of the ball.

# Practice Game for Corner Kicks

(Same methods as are used for long throw-ins, figure 6.6)

## Pitch

One-third pitch with two full-size goals.

## Players

Fourteen—seven versus seven, including a goalkeeper on each team.

## Organization

The players involved in the corner-kick combination are all on the same team (the "dead-ball team"). The dead-ball team attacks toward the penalty area.

## Description

Normal play. If the dead-ball players are awarded a throw-in or corner kick, they take a corner kick.

## Scoring

A goal can only be scored from a volley—the first touch finishing with either the head or a volley. However, goals are acknowledged if they are scored from a correctly executed corner-kick combination.

## Variations

1. A halfway line is introduced. If the dead-ball team gains possession of the ball on the opposition's half, it is awarded a corner kick.
2. Scoring a goal earns another corner kick.

## Coaching Points

If more than six players are involved in the corner-kick combination, the coach may first select the most important players. Subsequently, the pitch can be extended and the rest of the players introduced. During corner kicks, the players on the dead-ball team must concentrate solely upon their own roles in the corner-kick combination and ignore the risk the team is taking by bringing lots of players forward. The scoring condition is set partly because there is a relatively high number of players gathered in a small area and partly because the chances of the ball going out of play increase. Variations 1 and 2 can be used to increase the number of corner kicks; however, to prevent the game from becoming too boring for the opposing team, corner kicks should not occur too often.

# Free Kicks

How and where a quick free kick can be executed depends on several circumstances. These include whether the free kick is direct or indirect and from where on the pitch the team takes the free kick.

## Taken Quickly

The players' attention and concentration are often reduced when the game is interrupted by a referee's whistle. This fact can be exploited by taking a free kick quickly. With a quick free kick, there is an opportunity to play the ball far into the opposition's half, bypassing the majority of opponents. As, according to the rule book, execution of a free kick need only wait for a sign from the referee and not necessarily a whistle signal, the team in possession can put the ball into play before the opposing players are back in position. This opportunity occurs in particular when an opponent has committed a minor offense against the player with the ball, who is quickly ready to get play going again. However, more serious offenses can also be utilized in order to put the ball back into play quickly, because the opponent will anticipate a pause.

A disturbance among the players on the defending team often characterizes a free kick outside the penalty area. The defenders set up the wall, they point and direct to secure the marking, and they are unsure how the free kick will be taken. The attacking team can exploit this by taking the free kick unexpectedly. It can occasionally be advantageous for the attackers to pretend they are not ready for the free kick to be taken.

## Normal Execution

Exploiting the pause when a free kick is awarded can also be tactically smart. This applies particularly if the team is running a practiced scenario. It is wise for the players involved to be allowed time to get focused. The interruption in the game can also be utilized to reorganize the team and playing positions, and perhaps restart the team's rhythm. For example, if the team has constantly been under pressure, the free kick offers the opportunity to slow the game down.

## Location of the Free Kick

In the defensive zone, the player who takes the free kick must quickly judge whether there is an opportunity to play a pass forward. If this is too risky, the player must then play a safe ball—that is, to the nearest unmarked team member. A long free kick from the defensive zone can be utilized in certain situations, but the player taking the free kick must be sure that many of his teammates have had time to get into positions that create both width and depth.

From the midfield zone, there ought to be several opportunities to send the ball in behind the defensive formation, which is generally positioned

In a line at the edge of the penalty area. Again, the positions of other team members must ensure both width and depth.

Wide free kicks close to the penalty area can be taken as crosses into the penalty area or as combinations, as described in the section on corner kicks. When in a favorable position outside the penalty area, the team can take a free kick either as a direct finish on goal or use a rehearsed combination. Choosing one or another type of free kick depends on the situation and the abilities of each player. If the team has one or more players with highly developed shooting or powerful finishing techniques—Brazilian player Roberto Carlos is an example—the team may choose mainly to shoot directly on goal. On those occasions, it is also important to sometimes allow other players to take the free kick or carry out free-kick combinations. Alternating the ways the team takes a free kick will be unexpected, and it can also come in handy in matches where the players who normally take free kicks are absent. Following are some requirements for the players and some examples of combinations in free kicks from outside the penalty area.

In free kicks from within the penalty area (indirect), it is usually appropriate to finish close to the spot from which the free kick is taken. The ball can, for example, be flicked up off the ground to the shooter, who then has the advantage of more easily being able to pass it over the defending players who are pushing forward.

### Free Kicks Just Outside the Penalty Area

Free kicks just outside the penalty area provide good goal-scoring opportunities, and it is worth spending time increasing the chances of scoring. The team can do this through systematic practice of free-kick combinations and, possibly, diversions to distract the opposition.

Free-kick combinations must be practiced until they become automatic. Timing between the players is especially crucial. The effectiveness of the free kick depends to a great extent on all the players knowing their roles and being capable of fulfilling them. Unsuccessful free-kick combinations can be frustrating for the players involved, and they put a strain on the team's mental equilibrium. One of the main requirements, therefore, is to spend as much time as is necessary practicing free-kick combinations. On the other hand, learning a free-kick combination does not generally demand a lot of time if the coach is well prepared and has a good idea of the situation in general, knowing what is to happen and in what order. An alternative approach to planning and practicing free-kick combinations is to let the players get together and decide which combinations should be used, and then try them out in practice.

Diversionary maneuvers can be effective when a free kick is taken from outside the penalty area. The opponents read and misunderstand the initial action and adapt their countering move for something other than what ultimately happens. That means the opponents will be taken by surprise, thus gaining time for the attack. A way of upsetting the opposition's concentration is to simulate carelessness and take actions that appear to have another purpose, suggesting that it will be some time before the free kick is taken. For example, the team can have a player by the ball while another player paces out the distance to the wall. At the fifth step, the player passes the ball over the wall to another team member, who breaks free.

It is often a good idea to limit the goalkeeper's chances of following the path of the ball after the first touch, as this decreases available reaction time. The team can, for example, place two players on the goalkeeper's side of the wall so as to block his or her view. Besides disturbing the goalkeeper, the two players are also in a good position for second balls. Immediately after the shot is taken, they should turn and run toward goal.

The more combinations, the greater the opportunity to take the opposition by surprise; however, demands on the players involved will increase correspondingly. We have provided a few examples of combinations the players can utilize in free-kick situations outside the penalty area, divided into combinations using fewer or more than three players. There is also an example of how the team can rehearse a free-kick combination.

## Free-Kick Combinations Outside the Penalty Area

Following are several examples of free-kick combinations. Examples 1 and 2 use two to three players. These create a chance of finishing for one of the players. Examples 3-5 use more than three players.

# Free Kicks 1

### Organization

Two players (numbers 6 and 7) stand close by the ball, while a player (9) is positioned alongside the ball four to five meters away. See figure 6.9.

### Description

Number 6 flicks the ball in the air to 7, who volleys it.

### Variation

Number 6 passes with the sole of his foot to 9, who finishes.

### Coaching Points

This free kick is best used when it is taken close to the edge of the penalty area. Numbers 6 and 7 must be close to each other (about one meter apart); otherwise there is a risk of the flick being imprecise or

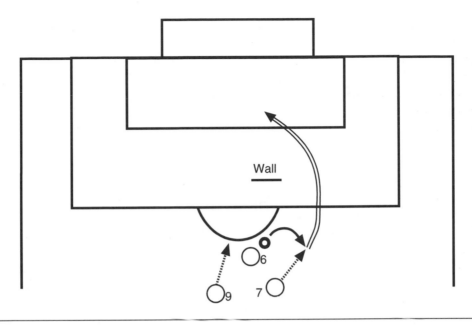

**Figure 6.9** Free kicks example 1.

of the opposition having the opportunity to get forward and block the shot. During the variation, 9 must simulate disinterest, possibly moving away from the free kick, and then suddenly turn around almost in the instant that 6 delivers the ball with the sole of his foot. The variation requires 6 to be able to pass with the sole of the foot extremely accurately.

# Free Kicks 2

### Organization

A player (number 8) stands behind the ball, while a player (9) sets up at the inner side of the wall. See figure 6.10.

### Description

Number 8 runs toward the ball and loops it over the wall to 9.

### Variation

Number 8 stands by the ball and pretends to intend sending the ball straight. Instead, 8 loops it over the wall.

### Coaching Points

The free kick is technically demanding for both 8 and 9; however, the combination can be effective since the area behind the wall is often

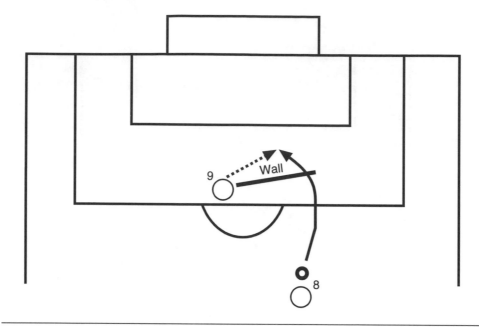

**Figure 6.10**   Free kicks example 2.

open. Number 9 must be positioned to face 8 and turn toward the wall in the instant that 8 arrives on the ball. Number 9 should, if possible, try to volley the ball; otherwise, there is a high risk of the defending players getting there and tackling.

# Free Kicks 3

### Organization

A player (number 7) stands by the ball, while two players (8 and 9) are positioned to the left of and behind the ball, and one player (2) stands back to the right of the ball. See figure 6.11.

### Description

Number 7 plays the ball across to 8, who fakes a shot and runs past the ball, so that 9 can finish.

### Variations

1. Number 8 finishes on goal.
2. Number 2 runs around 7 and receives an outside or heel pass from 7, after which 2 passes across to 9 or to another team member.
3. Another player (number 5) stops the ball for 9.

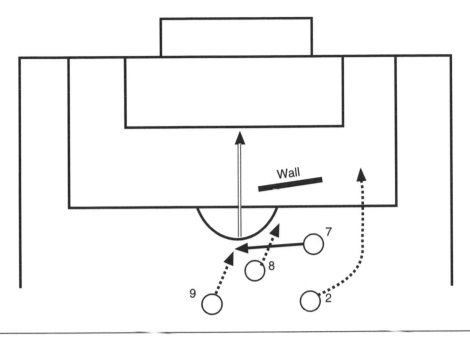

**Figure 6.11**    Free kicks example 3.

## Coaching Points

It is important for 8 to start the run in such a way that there is a realistic chance of finishing the ball. While rehearsing the combination, emphasis must be placed on keeping the passing angle and speed the same in every repetition, so that 8 and 9 know when they must start their run-up. Number 2 must start a moment before 7 passes the ball across to 8.

In variation 1, there should be no changes made to the runs or to the timing of when numbers 8 and 9 should start their runs.

During variation 2, number 2 should be able to run onto the pass from 7. In order to avoid the wall and receive the pass from 7, number 2 must make the run slightly away from the wall.

Variation 3 provides the advantage of 9 being given a "dead" ball beyond the reach of the wall. After stopping the ball, number 5 must quickly take two steps back.

## Free Kicks 4

Expansion of examples 1 and 3.

### Organization

A player (number 6) stands by the ball, two players (8 and 10) are positioned to the right of the ball, and three players (2, 7, and 9) are

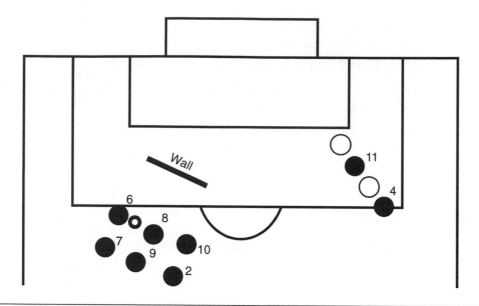

**Figure 6.12**   Free kicks example 4.

four to five meters behind the ball. Two players (4 and 11) stand in the penalty area opposite the ball. See figure 6.12.

## Description

Combination opportunities:

1. Number 7 shoots directly on goal, or else 6 flicks the ball off the ground to 7, who shoots on goal.
2. Number 6 plays 8, who controls the ball, and 9 shoots.
3. Number 6 passes to 8, who allows the ball to pass through his legs or stops the ball and passes it on with the sole of his foot, after which 10 stops it, and 2 finishes. Number 9 fakes a shot.
4. Number 6 or number 7 plays a high ball to 11 or 4.

The pass from 6 in combinations 2 through 4 can be taken either before or after 7 has jumped over the ball. On the right side of the field, the combination runs in the same manner, although some players often have to be switched (depending on whether they are left- or right-footed).

## Variations

1. Number 5 is a left-footed player who starts from the center of the field and makes a run toward the ball to the left of the wall. This gives the following opportunities for development:
   • A direct shot from 5

- A pass to 5 from either 6 or 7
- A pass to 5 over the wall from either 9 or 2

2. Numbers 2 and 10 are omitted from the combination.
3. Number 2 is omitted; number 7 finishes from 8's position, and 9 finishes from 10's position.
4. Number 9 can finish directly with his left foot or jump over the ball, whereupon 7 shoots from the original position of 6 or 8; or else, number 2 shoots from the original position of 8 or 10.

### Coaching Points

The combination must be performed rapidly so that the opposition will not be able to block the finishing shot. First, number 6 can fake a pass to see whether the opposition pushes up too quickly and to attract the referee's attention to the opposition encroaching on the 9.15 m free-kick rule. Combination 4 (see Description) and the second and third points in variation 1 can be effective if the opposition is pushing forward quickly. The only thing that, of necessity, must be agreed on the pitch is whether 7 should shoot at goal or leave the ball. Besides this, 9 may wish to know whether 8 is going to leave the ball or stop it for 9 to finish on goal.

During variation 1, number 5 must know whom to expect the pass from. If the ball is coming from the center of the pitch (2 and 9), number 5 must run across before moving in behind the wall. Also, the timing between the players is extremely important in this particular combination. Number 6 must make the pass immediately before or after 7 jumps over the ball (if 7 does so), 9 must start the run-up at around the time when 6 makes the pass, and 2 should start the run-up right after the ball has been passed on from 8.

# Free Kicks 5

### Organization

Two players (numbers 5 and 7) stand over the ball. One player (9) is positioned on the inner side of the wall. Three players (4, 10, and 11) take up positions beside each other at the corner of the penalty area opposite the spot from which the free kick is to be taken. See figure 6.13.

### Description

Combination options:

1. Number 5 shoots directly on goal with the left foot. Alternatively, 5 jumps over the ball and runs to the left of the wall.

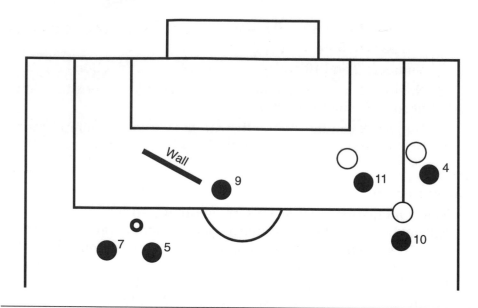

**Figure 6.13**   Free kicks example 5.

2. Number 7 plays 5, who dribbles toward the goal line and crosses the ball.

3. Number 7 shoots directly on goal.

4. Number 7 passes to 10, who runs along the edge of the penalty area toward the defensive wall. Number 10 passes with one touch to 9.

5. Number 7 sends a high ball to 4 or 11. If the free kick is executed on the right side of the field, numbers 5 and 7 switch roles.

6. Number 7 passes over the wall to 9.

### Coaching Points

This free-kick combination has the advantage that very little needs to be arranged on the pitch before the free kick is taken. It would be advisable for 5 to agree with 7 about the direct shot, although this is not absolutely necessary. The rest is up to 7—shoot on goal, or pass to 5, 10, 4, or 11? The other players do not need to be informed as to which of the combinations is to be utilized. They must all act as if they are directly involved in the combination being performed. The timing between 5, 7, and 10 is important. Number 7 must meet the ball at a time when there is the option of passing the ball on to 5's run, before 5 is caught offside. Number 10's run must wait until 7 moves toward the ball.

# Sample Free-Kick Combination Practice Session

The team can rehearse the free-kick combination in example 5 (pages 115-116) in the five phases discussed here.

## Phase One

Numbers 5 and 7 should first practice shooting from different positions around artificial or imaginary walls. After this, they rehearse the timing of when 7 should start the run and the ensuing pass to 5 on the left. The emphasis will be on 5's avoidance of an offside position (in relation to the wall, which can be marked by cones) and on 7 not passing too early, allowing the last player in the defensive wall to interfere. Number 5's run should be in an appropriate curve around the wall. The ball passes between 5 and the wall. The combination is also practiced on the right, where 5's and 7's roles are reversed.

## Phase Two

Numbers 9 and 10 join the practice; so does a defender who marks 10. The first run-through should concentrate on 10's run in relation to 7. Number 10 should be patient, so that there is space to pass to 9. After simulating disinterest, possibly moving out a little toward the sidelines, 10 should at the right moment turn and sprint along the edge of the penalty area. Number 7 should also be patient, so that 10 can come to pass in front of 9. During the first run-through, only the new aspects of the free kick are used. After that, the variants of phase one are merged in. The last part focuses on the players' roles once the actual combinations are completed. For example, 9 and 10 should make themselves available in front of the goal once 5 has received the ball at the side. After one side has been rehearsed to perfection, work is switched to the other side of the pitch.

## Phase Three

Numbers 4 and 11 are added, plus two defenders who mark them. After the introductory part of the free-kick combination has been completed as normal, this phase introduces crosses to 4 and 11 from 7. Aside from pass placement, attention should be paid to the roles of the other players once the free kick has been taken. What should 4 or 11 do on receiving the ball—head or pass toward goal, or across to 9, or possibly 10? After this, the first combination options are repeated and developed systematically, focusing additionally on the roles of 4 and 11 in these combinations.

## Phase Four

The players (that is, numbers 5 and 7) may decide for themselves which combination is to be used. The defenders start off relatively passively, but can quickly become fully active as appropriate. They should fulfill their marking roles and avoid exploiting their knowledge of the combination.

The free kick just outside the penalty area is a good scoring chance if the team is well prepared.

Eventually, two more defenders, who become the widest players in the wall, are introduced. After the free kick has been taken, they should mark numbers 5 and 9. In this phase, it can also be a good idea to introduce a goalkeeper. The free-kick model is carried out now as if it were a match; however, 5 and 7 may not shoot through the imaginary wall.

### Phase Five

The free-kick combination outside the penalty area is used in a game.

## Practice Game for Free Kicks

**Pitch**

About two-fifths pitch with two full-size goals.

**Players**

Fourteen—seven versus seven, one of whom on each team is a goalkeeper.

## Organization

The players involved in the free-kick combination are on the same team (the "dead-ball team"). The dead-ball team attacks toward the penalty area. See figure 6.14.

## Description

Normal play; however, the opposition may not pass to the goalkeeper, and the ball may not be played backward. If the opposition does either, the dead-ball team is awarded a free kick outside the penalty area.

## Scoring

Goals may only be scored from a one-touch finish of either a header or a volley. A goal is, however, acknowledged when it follows the use of the desired free-kick combination.

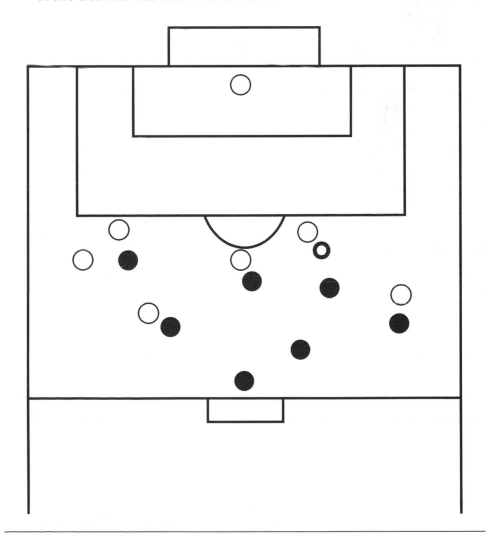

**Figure 6.14**    Free-kick practice.

## Variations

1. A halfway line is introduced. If the dead-ball players are awarded a throw-in on the opposition's half of the pitch, or a corner kick, they take a free kick outside the penalty area.

2. A goal gives the dead-ball team a free kick outside the penalty area.

## Coaching Points

If more than six players are involved in the free-kick combination, the most important players can be selected during the first run-through. Then the pitch can be widened and the remaining players brought in. The players on the dead-ball team should, during every free kick, concentrate solely on their roles in the combination and ignore the risk the team is running by bringing many players forward. To avoid doubt and ensure that the players shoot from different positions, the coach can set the rule that the free kick should be taken level with where the infraction was committed.

Variations 1 and 2 can be used to increase the number of free-kick opportunities, but to prevent play from becoming too trivialized for the opposing team, dead-ball situations should not occur too often.

In variations 1 and 2, the coach should clearly indicate where the free kick should be taken from, to create as realistic a situation as possible and avoid unnecessary confusion among the players.

# Penalty Kicks

A penalty kick gives the team an open opportunity for scoring a goal, but there are, nevertheless, quite a number of occasions when no goal is scored in these situations. For example, at the 1996 European Championships, 42 penalty kicks were taken and 37 were successful. A penalty kick puts great mental strain on the player who is to take it.

A player must meet some fundamental requirements in order to fulfill expectations and score from a penalty. One is to be calm when taking the penalty kick. That means the player puts the ball on the penalty spot and follows any personal routine in preparation for taking the kick. The player must ignore any irritations the goalkeeper may attempt (off-center positioning in the goal, perhaps, or dragging out preparation time) and must make and stick to the decision of where to place the ball, and how to strike it.

It is vital for the player to have rehearsed and developed the penalty finish. It is a good idea to be ready with several ways of striking the ball; however, it is crucial that, before placing the ball on the spot, the player decides how and where to shoot and sticks to this decision regardless of outside factors. The goalkeeper will normally observe the player's run-up and leg position in order to predict where the ball will arrive. The player taking the penalty kick should, therefore, not signal his intentions too clearly, unless he is faking.

The two most common types of penalties are to place the ball by the post, slightly above the ground, and to shoot hard without aiming anywhere in particular. In order to place the ball confidently just inside the post, the push-pass may be used. The run-up must be such that it is possible to shoot to both sides. A right-footed player will gain from taking an angled run-up to the left of the ball, and vice versa for a left-footed player. If the goalkeeper seems to know how the player tends to take penalties and is expecting a low shot, the ball can be sent up into the corner of the goal.

A player who uses the driven penalty bases the choice on the assumption that the goalkeeper will not have time to react. The goalkeeper often moves before the ball is played, which decreases the chances of saving a driven shot. The instep finish is the only possible kicking form in this type of penalty.

Because the mental aspect plays such a large part in penalty situations in league matches, it can be difficult to recreate in training the atmosphere of a penalty kick in match play. It is appropriate to have at least two established penalty takers on a team. As preparation for cup matches and international tournaments, more players should be trained in how to cope with the situation. A session aiming at the systematic training of penalty shooting consists of three phases, repeated at appropriate intervals. The first phase consists of the player's decision as to which type of shot to use. This can be performed in shooting practice. Areas in a goal can be marked so that the player can assess and adjust shot placement in relation to the initial intention. Set cones in the goal close to the posts as aiming points for low shots. Put cones or training vests in the top corners of the goal to act as accuracy checks on the rehearsed shots. The players work in pairs, and the player taking the penalty must, before finishing, let the other know the target. Various individual competitions can be devised, but it is vital to maintain a connection between the shot's power and position.

The second phase is the one the players will enjoy most, because it introduces the goalkeeper. It is also here that the training can easily lose its effectiveness, since the players cannot help trying to trick their own goalkeeper instead of keeping to the development of their penalty taking. Practicing penalty kicks with the goalkeeper requires tight organization. The coach must allow some time between finishes, both to give the keeper time to be ready and to put pressure on the penalty taker through the fact that the other players can watch.

The third is the test phase. Another goalkeeper, who has not previously been involved in the penalty taking (for example, the goalkeeper from the second or youth team), gets to play. In this phase, the game on pages 118-120 can be used. Besides that, normal training can end with a penalty shoot-out between the two teams, with the new goalkeeper in the goal. Each player has only one shot.

Repeat and adjust the three phases at intervals, depending on approaching challenges and changes in the group of penalty takers.

# Defense

Besides being well prepared for its own dead-ball situations, a team must work on defense to handle dead-ball situations from the opposition.

The defending players must quickly sum up the situation around the area where the infraction occurred and take appropriate defensive positions in relation to the ball. There should be prearranged and rehearsed routines as to roles in dead-ball situations. This allows the individual players more opportunity to concentrate on their own parts of the defensive task in a given dead-ball situation.

## Free Kicks

In situations where the opposition has a reasonable chance of finishing, the defending team must prevent the direct shot by setting up a line of players between the goal and the spot where the infraction took place: a wall. The wall can be set up according to the following guidelines:

• Decide beforehand who is to stand in the wall, and where each player is positioned in relation to the others.

• The wall should have about five players, and the tallest should be in the widest position. This position is determined by the next player, who stands in line with the ball and the near post. This means that the widest player in the wall stands about one meter outside the near post, to cover passes chipped over the wall and into the top corner of the near post (see figure 6.15).

• The goalkeeper should advise the second-widest player as to position, from the near post.

• The goalkeeper covers the far corner, positioned to see the spot from which the free kick is taken. The players in the wall must stand close enough together so that the ball cannot get through, and they should remain standing in the wall. At an elite level, one often sees several players in the wall jump in anticipation of the ball being played, at which point the ball is shot low under the wall and into goal.

• A player (a "killer") may be placed next to the wall on the same side the shot will come from. As soon as the ball is touched, this player moves rapidly forward toward the delivery, to try and block the shot.

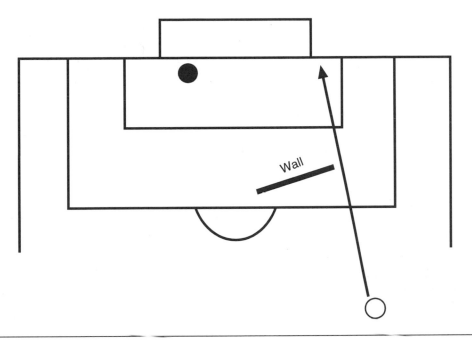

**Figure 6.15** Set up a wall.

If the players in the wall jump, as illustrated here by the German national side in the European Championship quarter-final against Croatia, they risk the ball being kicked straight under the wall.

In free kicks taken farther away from the penalty area, the wall becomes less important. But the wall can cover the direct shot on goal and be mentally disruptive to the player taking the free kick. The wall will usually consist of two players; however, the goalkeeper should decide the number of players needed there. This is also the case when the free kick is taken from a wide position in relation to the goal. If the player taking the free kick takes a long run-up, the defending team may place a player 9.15 meters behind the ball, in the path of the finishing player, in order to create distraction in the run-up.

## Throw-Ins

Players often lose concentration when the ball goes out for a throw-in. It is therefore vital to impress upon them that they should quickly take up the correct defensive positions. On a throw-in to the opposition, the nearest defenders should position themselves between their direct opponents and their own goal at a distance of about one meter, so they can both follow the opponents' moves and be covered if the ball is thrown to their direct opponent. Whoever throws the ball in should also be covered, since this player will otherwise be available to receive a pass following the throw. The defender marking the thrower should stand at a distance of three to five meters away. In the instant the ball is thrown, the defender should move toward and mark the player taking the throw-in.

On long throw-ins, two players may be used to cover the player who is to lengthen the ball's traveling distance (see figure 6.16). One defender takes position about one meter in front of the opponent, while another defender stands in the normal marking position behind this player: a so-

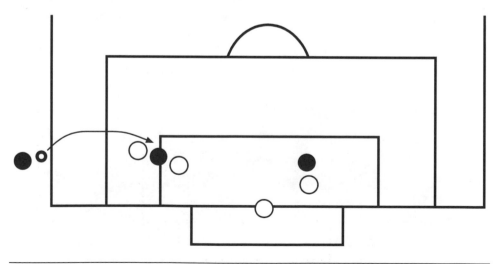

**Figure 6.16**  Use two defenders to cover the opponent who will lengthen the ball's traveling distance.

called "sandwich" formation. The defender in front should jump up and try to head the ball away—also restricting the opponent's view. The defender in back should push the opponent forward and try to get a good jump up for a header.

A defender can be positioned on the sideline, level with the player taking the throw-in, to force the opponent to send the ball up higher, thereby increasing the defense's chances of getting a head to the ball.

## Corner Kicks

In corner kicks, the goalkeeper should direct the area in front of the goal. This player is responsible for airborne balls in the goal area, apart from balls to the first part of the goal vicinity (see figure 6.17). To help out, it is often a good idea to position a player 9.15 meters from the corner flag (number 2). Such positioning will force the player taking the corner to pass higher and less directly, giving the goalkeeper a little extra time to read the path of the ball. Placing a player tight by the corner flag also makes it more difficult for the opposition to use a short corner. If the opposition chooses to take a short corner, the nearest defender should break toward that area to aid teammates who are already there. The goalkeeper (number 1) can take a position in the center of the goal, with legs slightly bent and upper body slightly turned in the direction of the player taking the corner. Thus, the goalkeeper can always see what is going on in most of the penalty area. This position will make it easier to come forward and out onto the pitch, as well as to move backward.

It is appropriate to have a defender (number 3) positioned in line with, and about one-half meter from, the near post. This player's task is to take

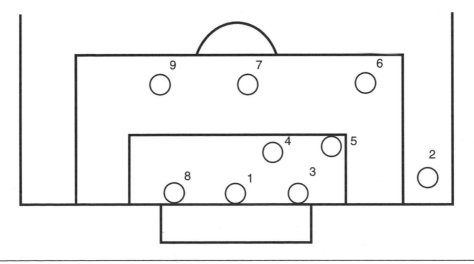

**Figure 6.17** The goalkeeper directs the area in front of the goal.

away the hard cross swerving inside toward the near post. If the opposition is preparing to lengthen the corner from the near post, this can be the further back of the two defenders who normally form a "sandwich" with the opposition's "lengthening" player.

Likewise, a defender (number 5) can be positioned in the near area of the goal, to look out for low inward balls swerving inside and players breaking forward. When the corner is taken to the back part of the penalty area, this player should move quickly to intervene if the ball is played across. If the opposition has a player close to the goalkeeper, one more player (number 4) can be placed in the goal area. The defender should stand beside the goalkeeper, not in front; that would impede the goalkeeper's forward movement should a ball come to the near area.

In the area farther back, defenders should take measures in case of long corners. If the opposition has players who are strong in the air there, it would be a good idea to have a player (number 8) at the far post. Otherwise, it can be sufficient to have the back defender nearer to the line of the goal area.

The other players should stand so that the most dangerous areas are covered most tightly. Their positions should be based on the opposition's formation and moves. The coach may also choose to let one or two defenders man-mark the players from the opposing team who are strongest in the air.

## Penalty Kicks

The team's fastest players should position themselves where the "D" crosses the line of the penalty area. When the penalty is taken, they should be the first to get a possible second ball away from the penalty area.

# Conclusion

Many goals, often spectacular ones, come from dead-ball situations, and they enrich the game and the aesthetic experience of the game. Soccer enthusiasts collect such experiences, where rehearsed combinations succeed. One such example is Thomas Brolin's goal during the 1994 World Cup in the match against Romania, where he runs diagonally behind the wall and is played deep in the opposition's penalty area, after which he finishes with a hard, high instep volley. A wonderful detail of high quality, created by personal courage and systematic teamwork. Often, the time needed to practice a dead-ball combination is very limited, but the rewards can be substantial. It can, therefore, be extremely useful, regardless of the level of soccer, to work with dead-ball situations.

# ABOUT THE AUTHORS

**Jens Bangsbo** has been playing and coaching soccer for more than 35 years. He spent 15 years as a top-level player in Denmark, playing more than 400 matches in the top Danish league. In international play, he represented Denmark as both a youth player and as a member of the "A" national team.

Bangsbo is a regular teacher at UEFA and FIFA courses. He is the advisor to the Danish national teams and to Juventus FC. An instructor at the Danish Football Association since 1986, Bangsbo has published more than 100 articles on soccer and conditioning, and he has written *Fitness Training in Football—A Scientific Approach*.

**Birger Peitersen** is also one of Denmark's top soccer figures, having coached the Danish Women's National Team and the national champions of the men's league, and also serving as staff coach of the Danish Football Federation. In 1982, he received the highest coaching award in Denmark, the Diploma in Elite Soccer Coaching.

Peitersen is the expert commentator for International European Matches on Danish television in the UEFA Champions League and for Danish Radio covering the World Cup in 1990 and 1998 and the European Championships in 1992 and 1996.

# Kick your program into high gear!

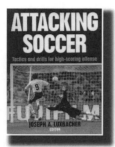
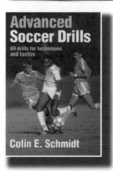